Lectionary

Advent 2010 to the eve of Advent 2011 (Year A)

Church House Publishing

Published by	Church House Publishing Church House Great Smith Street London SW1P 3AZ
Compilation ©	*The Archbishops' Council 2010*
ISBN	978-0-7151-2166-5 (standard) 978-0-7151-2167-2 (large)

Authorization	The Common Worship Calendar and Lectionaries are authorized pursuant to Canon B 2 of the Canons of the Church of England for use until further resolution of the General Synod of the Church of England.

Copyright and Acknowledgements	*The Revised Common Lectionary* is copyright © The Consultation on Common Texts: 1992. The Church of England adaptations to the Principal Service Lectionary are copyright © The Archbishops' Council, as are the Second and Third Service Lectionaries and the Weekday Lectionary for Morning and Evening Prayer.

The Daily Eucharistic Lectionary derives, with some adaptation, from the *Ordo Lectionum Missae* of the Roman Catholic Church and is reproduced by permission of The International Commission on English in the Liturgy.

Edited by Jonathan Goodall
Designed by Derek Birdsall & John Morgan/Omnific
Typeset by RefineCatch Ltd, Bungay, Suffolk
Printed in England by Core Publications

How to use this book

This booklet gives details of the full range of
possibilities envisaged in the liturgical calendar and
lectionary of Common Worship. Its use as a tool for
the preparation of worship will require the making
of several choices based first on the general
celebration of the Christian year by the Church of
England as a whole; second on the customary
pattern of calendar in the diocese, parish and place
of worship; and third on the pattern of services
locally.

The **first column** comprises the Calendar of the
Church with the days of the year. Observances that
are mandatory are printed either in **bold** type
(Sundays), in **bold** type (Principal Feasts and Holy
Days) or in roman (Festivals). Optional celebrations
(Lesser Festivals) and Commemorations are printed
in ordinary roman type and *italic* type respectively.

The **second column** comprises (a) the readings and
psalms for the Principal Service on Sundays, Principal
Feasts and Holy Days, and Festivals, and (b) Holy
Communion readings and psalms for other days of
the week. On the Sundays after Trinity, the Old
Testament reading and its psalm are divided into two
smaller columns, indicating a choice between a
'continuous' reading week by week or a reading
'related' to the Gospel for that day.

The **third column** comprises (a) the Third Service
readings and psalms for Sundays, Principal Feasts and
Holy Days, and Festivals, and (b) the readings and
psalms for weekday Morning Prayer.

The **fourth column** comprises (a) the Second
Service readings and psalms for Sundays, Principal
Feasts and Holy Days, and Festivals, and (b) the
readings and psalms for weekday Evening Prayer.

Sundays, Principal Feasts and Holy Days and Festivals

Three sets of psalms and readings are provided for each Sunday, Principal Feast or Holy Day and Festival.

The **Principal Service lectionary** (based on the Revised Common Lectionary) is intended for use at the principal service of the day (whether this service is Holy Communion or some other authorized form). In most Church communities, this is likely to be the mid-morning service, but the minister is free to decide which service time normally constitutes the Principal Service of the day. This lectionary may be used twice if required – for example, at an early celebration of Holy Communion and then again at a later one.

If only **two readings** are used at the Principal Service and that service is Holy Communion, the second reading must always be the Gospel reading. When the Principal Service lectionary is used at a service other than Holy Communion, the Gospel reading need not always be chosen.

The **Second Service lectionary** is intended for a second main service. In many churches, this lectionary may be the appropriate provision for a Sunday afternoon or evening service. A Gospel reading is always provided so that this lectionary can, if necessary, be used where the second main service is a celebration of Holy Communion.

The **Third Service lectionary**, with shorter readings, is intended where a third set of psalms and readings is needed and is most appropriate for use at an office. A Gospel reading is not always provided, so this lectionary is not suitable for use at Holy Communion.

Weekdays

The Common Worship Weekday Lectionary authorized by the General Synod in 2005 comprises a lectionary (with psalms) for Holy Communion, a lectionary for Morning and Evening Prayer, and tables of psalms for Morning and Evening Prayer.

The **Daily Eucharistic Lectionary** (based on the Roman Catholic daily eucharistic lectionary) is a semi-continuous two-year lectionary with a wide use of scripture, though not complete coverage of the Bible. Two readings are provided for each day, the first from either the Old or New Testament, the second always a Gospel. Psalm provision is intended to be a brief response to the first reading. It is for use at Holy Communion normally in places with a daily or near-daily celebration with a regular congregation. It may also be used as an office lectionary.

The **lectionary for Morning and Evening Prayer** always provides two readings for each office, the first from the Old Testament and the second from the New Testament. These are generally in sequence. One of the New Testament readings for any particular day is from the Gospels.

In Ordinary Time (apart from the period from All Saints to the beginning of Advent) the **psalms for Morning and Evening Prayer** follow a sequential pattern.

In the periods from All Saints until 18 December, from the Epiphany until the Presentation of Christ in the Temple (Candlemas), from Ash Wednesday until Palm Sunday, and from the Monday after Easter Week until Pentecost, there is a choice of psalms at Morning and Evening Prayer. The psalms printed first reflect the theme of the season. Alternatively, the psalms from the Ordinary Time cycle may be used. The two sets are separated by 'or'.

From 19 December until the Epiphany and from the Monday of Holy Week until the Saturday of Easter Week, only seasonal psalms are provided.

Where more than one psalm is given, one psalm (printed in **bold**) may be used as the sole psalm at that office.

Guidance on how these options for saying the psalms are expressed typographically can be found in the 'Notes on the Lectionary' below.

A further cycle is provided (see table on page 79), which is largely the monthly sequential cycle of psalms given in the *Book of Common Prayer*.

A single psalm for use by those who only say one office each day is provided in Prayer During the Day in *Common Worship: Daily Prayer*.

Liturgical colours

Colours are indicated by single letters: the first (always upper case) for the season or Festival; and occasionally a second (lower case) for an optional celebration on that day. Thus, for example, *Gr* for the celebration of a Lesser Festival whose liturgical colour is red, in an otherwise 'green' season.

Common of the Saints

General readings and psalms for saints' days can be found on pages 72–76; for some particular celebrations, other readings are suggested there.

Special Occasions

Readings and psalms for special occasions can be found on pages 72–78.

Notes on the Calendar 28 November 2010– 26 November 2011

These notes are based on the Rules to Order the Christian Year (*Common Worship: Times and Seasons*, pages 24–30).

Sundays

All Sundays celebrate the paschal mystery of the death and resurrection of the Lord. They also reflect the character of the seasons in which they are set.

Principal Feasts

On these days (printed in bold) Holy Communion is celebrated in every cathedral and parish church, and this celebration, required by Canon B 14, may not be displaced by any other celebration, and may only be dispensed with in accordance with the provision of Canon B 14A.

Except in the case of Christmas Day and Easter Day, the celebration of the Feast *begins with Evening Prayer on the day before the Feast,* and the Collect at that Evening Prayer is that of the Feast. In the case of Christmas Eve and Easter Eve, there is proper liturgical provision (including a Collect) for the whole day.

The Epiphany may, for pastoral reasons, be celebrated on Sunday 2 January. **The Presentation of Christ in the Temple** (Candlemas) is celebrated on either Wednesday 2 February or Sunday 30 January. **All Saints' Day** may be celebrated on Sunday 30 October, replacing the Fourth Sunday before Advent.

Other Principal Holy Days

These days (printed in bold), and the liturgical provision for them, may not be displaced by any other celebration.

Ash Wednesday (9 March) and **Maundy Thursday** (21 April) are Principal Holy Days. On both these days Holy Communion is celebrated in every cathedral or parish church, except where there is dispensation under Canon B 14A.

Good Friday (22 April) is a Principal Holy Day.

Eastertide

The paschal character of **the Great Fifty Days of Easter**, from Easter Day (24 April) to Pentecost (12 June), should be celebrated throughout the season, and should not be displaced by other celebrations.

Except for a Patronal or Dedication Festival, no Festival may displace the celebration of a Sunday in Eastertide, as a memorial of the resurrection and no saint's day may be celebrated in Easter Week. The paschal character of the season should be retained on those weekdays when saints' days are celebrated.

The three days before Ascension Day (30 May–1 June) are customarily observed as **Rogation Days**, when prayer is offered for God's blessing on the fruits of the earth and on human labour.

The nine days **after Ascension Day until the eve of Pentecost** (3–11 June) are observed as days of prayer and preparation for the celebration of the outpouring of the Holy Spirit.

Festivals

These days (printed in roman), and the liturgical provision for them, are not usually displaced. For each day there is full liturgical provision for a Principal, Second and Third Service, and an optional so-called First Evening Prayer on the evening before the Festival where this is required.

Festivals may *not* be celebrated on Sundays in Advent, Lent or Eastertide, the Baptism of Christ, Ascension Day, Trinity Sunday or Christ the King, or weekdays between Palm Sunday and the Second Sunday of Easter. A Festival coinciding with these days is transferred to the first available day: hence George is transferred from 23 April (Easter Eve) to 2 May, Mark is transferred from 25 April (Monday in Easter Week) to 3 May, and Philip and James is transferred from 1 May (Second Sunday of Easter) to 4 May. Otherwise, Festivals falling on a Sunday — namely in 2011 Thomas the Apostle on the Second Sunday after Trinity — may be kept on that Sunday or transferred to the Monday (or, at the discretion of the minister, to the next suitable weekday).

Certain Festivals (namely, Matthias the Apostle, the Visit of the BVM to Elizabeth, Thomas the Apostle, and the Blessed Virgin Mary) have customary alternative dates (see page 8).

The Thursday after Trinity Sunday (23 June) may be observed as the **Day of Thanksgiving for the Institution of Holy Communion** (sometimes known as *Corpus Christi*), and may be kept as a Festival.

Other Celebrations

Mothering Sunday falls on 3 April, the Fourth Sunday of Lent. Alternative prayers and readings are provided for the Principal Service.

Bible Sunday may be celebrated on 23 October, replacing the Last Sunday after Trinity, and appropriate prayers and readings are provided.

Local Celebrations

The celebration of **the patron saint or the title of a church** is kept either as a Festival or as a Principal Feast.

The **Dedication Festival** of a church is the anniversary of the date of its dedication or consecration. This is kept either as a Festival or as a Principal Feast. When kept as Principal Feasts, the Patronal and Dedication Festivals may be transferred to the nearest Sunday, unless that day is already a Principal Feast or one of the following days: the First Sunday of Advent, the Baptism of Christ, the First Sunday of Lent, the Fifth Sunday of Lent, or Palm Sunday. If the actual date is not known, the Dedication Festival may be celebrated on 2 October (replacing the Fifteenth Sunday after Trinity), or 23 October (replacing the Last Sunday after Trinity), or on a suitable date chosen locally. Readings can be found on page 71.

Harvest Thanksgiving may be celebrated on any Sunday in autumn, replacing the provision for that day, provided it does not displace any Principal Feast or Festival.

Diocesan and other local provision may be made in **the calendar of the saints** to supplement the general calendar, in accordance with Canon B 6, paragraph 5.

Lesser Festivals

Lesser Festivals (printed in ordinary roman type, in black) are observed in a manner appropriate to a particular place. Each is provided with a Collect, which may supersede the Collect of the week. For certain Lesser Festivals a complete set of Eucharistic readings is provided, and for others appropriate readings may be selected from the Common of the Saints (see pages 72–76) These readings may, at the minister's discretion, supersede the Daily Eucharistic Lectionary (DEL). The weekday Psalms and Readings at Morning and Evening Prayer are not usually superseded by those for Lesser Festivals, but at the minister's discretion Psalms and Readings provided on these days for use at Holy Communion may be used instead at Morning or Evening Prayer.

The minister may be selective in the Lesser Festivals that are observed and may also keep some, or all of them, as Commemorations, perhaps especially in Advent, Lent and Paschaltide where the character of the season ought to be sustained. If the Day of Thanksgiving for the Institution of Holy Communion (23 June) is not kept as a Festival, it may be kept as a Lesser Festival.

When a Lesser Festival falls on a Principal Feast or Holy Day, a Festival, a Sunday, or on a weekday between Palm Sunday and the Second Sunday of Easter, its celebration is normally omitted for that year. However, where there is sufficient reason, it may, at the discretion of the minister be celebrated on the nearest available day.

Commemorations

Commemorations (printed in *italic*) are made by a mention in prayers of intercession. They are not provided with Collect, Psalm and Readings, and do not replace the usual weekday provision at Holy Communion or at Morning and Evening Prayer.

The minister may be selective in the Commemorations that are made.

Only where there is an established celebration in the wider Church or where the day has a special local significance may a Commemoration be observed as a Lesser Festival, with liturgical provision from the Common of the Saints (pages 72–76).

In designating a Commemoration as a Lesser Festival, the minister must remember the need to maintain the spirit of the season, especially of Advent, Lent and Eastertide.

Days of Discipline and Self-Denial

The weekdays of Lent and every Friday in the year are days of discipline and self-denial, with the exception of Principal Feasts, Festivals outside Lent, and Fridays from Easter Day to Pentecost. The day preceding a Principal Feast may also be appropriately kept as a day of discipline and self-denial in preparation for the Feast.

Ember Days

Ember Days should be kept, under the bishop's directions, in the week before an ordination as days of prayer for those to be ordained deacon or priest.

Ember Days may also be kept even when there is no ordination in the diocese as more general days of prayer for those who serve the Church in its various ministries, both ordained and lay, and for vocations. Traditionally they have been observed on the Wednesday, Friday and Saturday in the week before the Third Sunday of Advent, the Second Sunday of Lent, and the Sundays nearest to 29 June and 29 September.

Ordinary Time

Ordinary Time comprises two periods in the year: first, the period from the day after the Presentation of Christ in the Temple until the day before Ash Wednesday, and second, that from the day after Pentecost until the day before the First Sunday of Advent.

During Ordinary Time, there is no seasonal emphasis, except that the period between All Saints' Day and the First Sunday of Advent is observed as a time to celebrate and reflect upon the reign of Christ in earth and heaven.

Liturgical Colours

Appropriate liturgical colours are suggested in this booklet. They are not mandatory; traditional or local use may be followed.

Notes on the Lectionary

The Sunday and festal readings for 28 November 2010 (the First Sunday of Advent) to 26 November 2011 (the eve of Advent) are from **Year A**, which offers a semi-continuous reading of Matthew's Gospel at the Principal Service on Sundays throughout the year.

The weekday readings for Holy Communion are from **Year One** of the Daily Eucharistic Lectionary (DEL).

Office readings are from Table 2 of the Weekday Lectionary: at Morning Prayer, Old Testament 2a and New Testament 2; and at Evening Prayer, Old Testament 1 and New Testament 1.

All **Bible references** (except to the Psalms) are to the *New Revised Standard Version* (New York, 1989). Those who use other Bible translations should check the verse numbers against the *NRSV*. Each reference gives book, chapter and verse, in that order.

References to the psalms are to the Common Worship psalter, published in *Common Worship: Services and Prayers for the Church of England* (2000) and *Common Worship: Daily Prayer* (2005). A table showing the verse number differences between this and the psalter in the *Book of Common Prayer* is provided on the Common Worship web site (http://www.cofe.anglican.org/commonworship).

Options in the provision of readings or psalms are presented in the following ways:

¶ square brackets [xx] give either optional additional verses or psalms, or a shorter alternative;

¶ 'or' indicates a simple choice between two alternative readings or courses of psalms;

¶ a psalm printed in **bold** may be used as the sole psalm at that office;

¶ on weekdays a psalm printed in parentheses (xx) is omitted if it has been used as the opening canticle at that office;

¶ a psalm marked with an asterisk may be shortened if desired.

Where a reading from the **Apocrypha** is offered, an alternative Old Testament reading is provided.

In the choice of **readings other than the Gospel** reading, the minister should ensure that, in any year, a balance is maintained between readings from the Old and New Testaments and that, where a particular biblical book is appointed to be read over several weeks, the choice ensures that the continuity of one book is not lost.

On the Sundays after Trinity, the Principal Service Lectionary provides **alternative Old Testament readings and psalms**. References in the left-hand column (under the heading 'Continuous') offer a *semi-continuous* reading of Old Testament texts. Such a reading and its complementary psalmody stand independently of the other readings. References in the right-hand column (under the heading 'Related') *relate* the Old Testament reading and the psalm to the Gospel reading. One column should be followed for the whole sequence of Sundays after Trinity.

Notes on Collects

For a table showing where the Collects and Post Communions are published, see page 71.

Where a Collect ends 'through Jesus Christ ... now and for ever', the minister may omit the longer (trinitarian) ending and use the shorter ending, 'through Jesus Christ our Lord', to which the people respond, 'Amen'. The longer ending, however, is to be preferred at a service of Holy Communion.

The Collect for each Sunday is used at Evening Prayer on the Saturday preceding, except where that Saturday is a Principal Feast, or a Festival, or the eve of Christmas Day or Easter Day. The Collect for each Sunday is also used on the weekdays following, except where other provision is made.

Abbreviations used in this book

Alt Alternative
Bp Bishop
BVM Blessed Virgin Mary
Cant Canticle
Comps Companions
DEL Daily Eucharistic Lectionary
EP Evening Prayer
G Green

HC Holy Communion: used where additional references are given to provide alternative texts for use at a celebration of Holy Communion (most often the provision of a psalm or gospel)
Mm Martyrs
MP Morning Prayer

P or p Purple or Violet
P(La) Purple or Lent Array
Ps & Pss Psalmody
R or r Red
Ss Saints
vv Verses: used where the source is not subdivided into chapters
W or w White (Gold is indicated where its use would be appropriate)

Eccles Ecclesiastes
Ecclus Ecclesiasticus
Sol Song of Solomon (also called Song of Songs)

Standard abbreviations have been used for other books of the Bible where necessary.

Alternative dates

The following may be celebrated on the alternative dates indicated:

Chad
– with Cedd on 26 October instead of 2 March

Matthias the Apostle
– on 24 February instead of 14 May

The Visit of the Blessed Virgin Mary to Elizabeth
– on 2 July instead of 31 May

Thomas the Apostle
– on 21 December instead of Sunday 3 July or Monday 4 July

The Blessed Virgin Mary
– on 8 September instead of 15 August

Thomas Becket
– on 7 July instead of 29 December

If any of these four festivals is celebrated on the alternative date these provisions should be used on the principal date:

Holy Communion	Morning Prayer	Evening Prayer
If Matthias the Apostle is celebrated on Thursday 24 February the following provision is used on Saturday 14 May (W):		
Acts 9.31–42	Psalms 108, 110, 111 or 41, **42**, 43	Psalms 23, **27** or 45, **46**
Psalm 116.10–15	Deuteronomy 8	Exodus 29.1–9
John 6.60–69	Ephesians 3.14–end	Luke 2.21–40
If The Visit of the Blessed Virgin Mary to Elizabeth is celebrated on Saturday 2 July the following provision is used on Tuesday 31 May (W):		
Acts 16.22–34	Psalms 124, 125, **126**, 127 or 87, **89.1–18**	Psalms **128**, 129, 130, 131 or **89.19–end**
Psalm 138	Deuteronomy 28.1–14	Numbers 16.36–end
John 16.5–11	1 Peter 4.12–end	Luke 6.39–end
If Thomas the Apostle is celebrated on Wednesday 21 December the following provision is used on Monday 4 July (G):		
Genesis 28.10–end	Psalm 44	Psalm 47, 49
Psalm 91.1–10	Ezra 1	Judges 2
Matthew 9.18–26	Romans 9.1–18	Luke 13.1–9
If The Blessed Virgin Mary is celebrated on Thursday 8 September the following provision is used on Monday 15 August (G):		
Judges 2.11–19	Psalms 27, **30**	Psalms 26, **28**, 29
Psalm 106.34–42	Jeremiah 31.23–25, 27–37	1 Samuel 14.24–46
Matthew 19.16–22	James 2.1–13	Luke 23.13–25

Key to the Tables

For guidance on how the options for saying the psalms are expressed typographically, see page 7.

Sundays (and Principal Feasts, other Principal Holy Days, and Festivals)

		Principal Service	3rd Service	2nd Service
Day	**Date**	Main service of the day:	Shorter Readings,	2nd main Service,
	Colour	Holy Communion, Morning Prayer,	an Office lectionary probably used at	probably used at Evening Prayer;
	Sunday / Feast † / Festival ††	Evening Prayer; or a Service of the	Morning Prayer where Holy	adaptable for Holy Communion
		Word	Communion is the Principal Service	

† Principal Feasts and other Principal Holy Days are printed in **bold**.
†† Festivals are printed in roman typeface.

Weekdays

		Holy Communion	Morning Prayer	Evening Prayer
Day	**Date**	Weekday readings	Psalms and readings for	Psalms and readings for
	Colour		Morning Prayer	Evening Prayer
	Lesser Festival ‡* [optional]			
	Commemoration ‡‡ [optional]			

‡ Lesser Festivals are printed in roman typeface, in black.
‡‡ Commemorations are printed in *italics*.
* The ascriptions given to holy men and women in the Calendar (such as martyr; teacher of the faith, etc.) have often been abbreviated in this booklet for reasons of space. The particular ascription given is there to be helpful if needing to choose Collects and readings from Common of the Saints; where several ascriptions are used (e.g. bishop and martyr), traditionally the last ascription given is the most important and therefore the guiding one. The full ascriptions may be found in the Calendar, which is printed in *Common Worship: Times and Seasons* (pages 7–22), *Common Worship: Festivals* (pages 5–20) and *Common Worship: Daily Prayer* (pages 5–16). These incorporate minor corrections made since the publication of the Calendar in *Common Worship: Services and Prayers for the Church of England* (pages 5–16).

9

	Principal Service	3rd Service	2nd Service
Sunday 28 November **1st Sunday of Advent** *P*	Isaiah 2.1–5 Psalm 122 Romans 13.11–end Matthew 24.36–44	Psalm 44 Micah 4.1–7 1 Thessalonians 5.1–11	Psalm 9 [or 9.1–8] Isaiah 52.1–12 Matthew 24.15–28
Monday 29 November *Day of Intercession and Thanksgiving for the Missionary Work of the Church* *P*	**Holy Communion** Isaiah 4.2–end Psalm 122 Matthew 8.5–11	**Morning Prayer** Psalms **50**, 54 or 1, 2, 3 Isaiah 42.18–end Revelation 19	**Evening Prayer** Psalms 70, **71** or **4**, 7 Isaiah 25.1–9 Matthew 12.1–21 or: 1st EP of Andrew the Apostle: Psalm 48; Isaiah 49.1–9a; 1 Corinthians 4.9–16
Tuesday 30 November Andrew the Apostle *R*	**Principal Service** Isaiah 52.7–10 Psalm 19.1–6 Romans 10.12–18 Matthew 4.18–22	**3rd Service** MP Psalms 47, 147.1–12 Ezekiel 47.1–12 or Ecclesiasticus 14.20–end John 12.20–32	**2nd Service** EP Psalms 87, 96 Zechariah 8.20–end John 1.35–42
Wednesday 1 December *Charles de Foucauld, hermit, 1916* *P*	**Holy Communion** Isaiah 25.6–10a Psalm 23 Matthew 15.29–37	**Morning Prayer** Psalms 5, 7 or **119.1–32** Isaiah 43.14–end Revelation 21.1–8	**Evening Prayer** Psalms 76, **77** or 11, 12, 13 Isaiah 28.1–13 Matthew 12.38–end
Thursday 2 December *P*	Isaiah 26.1–6 Psalm 118.18–27a Matthew 7.21, 24–27	Psalms 42, 43 or 14, **15**, 16 Isaiah 44.1–8 Revelation 21.9–21	Psalms **40**, 46 or **18*** Isaiah 28.14–end Matthew 13.1–23
Friday 3 December *Francis Xavier, missionary, 1552* *P*	Isaiah 29.17–end Psalm 27.1–4, 16–17 Matthew 9.27–31	Psalms 25, 26 or 17, **19** Isaiah 44.9–23 Revelation 21.22—22.5	Psalms 16, 17 or **22** Isaiah 29.1–14 Matthew 13.24–43
Saturday 4 December *John of Damascus, monk, teacher of the faith, c.749* *Nicholas Ferrar, deacon, founder of the Little Gidding Community, 1637* *P*	Isaiah 30.19–21, 23–26 Psalm 146.4–9 Matthew 9.35—10.1, 6–8	Psalms **9** (10) or 20, 21, **23** Isaiah 44.24—45.13 Revelation 22.6–end	Psalms **27**, 28 or 24, **25** Isaiah 29.15–end Matthew 13.44–end

		Principal Service	3rd Service	2nd Service
Sunday	**5 December** 2nd Sunday of Advent	*P* Isaiah 11.1–10 Psalm 72.1–7, 18–19 [or 72.1–7] Romans 15.4–13 Matthew 3.1–12	Psalm 80 Amos 7 Luke 1.5–20	Psalms 11 [28] 1 Kings 18.17–39 John 1.19–28
		Holy Communion	**Morning Prayer**	**Evening Prayer**
Monday	**6 December** Nicholas, bishop, c. 326 (see p. 74)	*Pw* Isaiah 35 Psalm 85.7–end Luke 5.17–26	Psalms **44** or 27, **30** Isaiah 45.14–end 1 Thessalonians 1	Psalms **144**, 146 or 26, **28**, 29 Isaiah 30.1–18 Matthew 14.1–12
Tuesday	**7 December** Ambrose, bishop, teacher of the faith, 397 (see p. 74)	*Pw* Isaiah 40.1–11 Psalm 96.1, 10–end Matthew 18.12–14	Psalms **56**, 57 or 32, **36** Isaiah 46 1 Thessalonians 2.1–12	Psalms 11, 12, 13 or **33** Isaiah 30.19–end Matthew 14.13–end
Wednesday	**8 December** Conception of the Blessed Virgin Mary (see p. 72) Ember Day	*Pw* Isaiah 40.25–end Psalm 103.8–13 Matthew 11.28–end	Psalms **62**, 63 or **34** Isaiah 47 1 Thessalonians 2.13–end	Psalms **10**, 14 or 119.33–**56** Isaiah 31 Matthew 15.1–20
Thursday	**9 December**	*P* Isaiah 41.13–20 Psalm 145.1, 8–13 Matthew 11.11–15	Psalms 53, **54**, 60 or **37*** Isaiah 48.1–11 1 Thessalonians 3	Psalms **73** or 39, **40** Isaiah 32 Matthew 15.21–28
Friday	**10 December** Ember Day	*P* Isaiah 48.17–19 Psalm 1 Matthew 11.16–19	Psalms 85, **86** or **31** Isaiah 48.12–end 1 Thessalonians 4.1–12	Psalms 82, **90** or **35** Isaiah 33.1–22 Matthew 15.29–end
Saturday	**11 December** Ember Day	*P* Ecclesiasticus 48.1–4, 9–11 or 2 Kings 2.9–12 Psalm 80.1–4, 18–19 Matthew 17.10–13	Psalms 145 or 41, **42**, 43 Isaiah 49.1–13 1 Thessalonians 4.13–end	Psalms 93, **94** or 45, **46** Isaiah 35 Matthew 16.1–12

11

	Principal Service	3rd Service	2nd Service
Sunday 12 December **3rd Sunday of Advent** P	Isaiah 35.1–10 Psalm 146.4–10 or Canticle: Magnificat James 5.7–10 Matthew 11.2–11	Psalm 68.1–19 Zephaniah 3.14–end Philippians 4.4–7	Psalms 12 [14] Isaiah 5.8–end Acts 13.13–41 HC John 5.31–40
	Holy Communion	**Morning Prayer**	**Evening Prayer**
Monday 13 December Pr Lucy, martyr, 304 (see p. 72) Samuel Johnson, moralist, 1784	Numbers 24.2–7, 15–17 Psalm 25.3–8 Matthew 21.23–27	Psalm **40** or **44** Isaiah 49.14–25 1 Thessalonians 5.1–11	Psalms 25, **26** or **47**, 49 Isaiah 38.1–8, 21–22 Matthew 16.13–end
Tuesday 14 December Pw John of the Cross, poet, teacher of the faith, 1591 (see p. 73)	Zephaniah 3.1–2, 9–13 Psalm 34.1–6, 21–22 Matthew 21.28–32	Psalms **70**, 74 or **48**, 52 Isaiah 50 1 Thessalonians 5.12–end	Psalms **50**, 54 or **50** Isaiah 38. 9–20 Matthew 17.1–13
Wednesday 15 December P	Isaiah 45.6b–8, 18, 21b–end Psalm 85.7–end Luke 7.18b–23	Psalms 75, 96 or 119.**57–80** Isaiah 51.1–8 2 Thessalonians 1	Psalms 25, **82** or **59**, 60 (67) Isaiah 39 Matthew 17.14–21
Thursday 16 December P	Isaiah 54.1–10 Psalm 30.1–5, 11–end Luke 7.24–30	Psalms **76**, 97 or 56, **57** (63*) Isaiah 51.9–16 2 Thessalonians 2	Psalms 44 or 61, **62**, 64 Zephaniah 1.1–2.3 Matthew 17.22–end
Friday 17 December P O Sapientia Eglantyne Jebb, social reformer, founder of 'Save The Children', 1928	Genesis 49.2, 8–10 Psalm 72.1–5, 18–19 Matthew 1.1–17	Psalms 77, **98** or **51**, 54 Isaiah 51.17–end 2 Thessalonians 3	Psalm 49 or **38** Zephaniah 3.1–13 Matthew 18.1–20
Saturday 18 December P	Jeremiah 23.5–8 Psalm 72.1–2, 12–13, 18–end Matthew 1.18–24	Psalm **71** or **68** Isaiah 52.1–12 Jude	Psalms 42, **43** or 65, **66** Zephaniah 3.14–end Matthew 18.21–end

	Principal Service	3rd Service	2nd Service
Sunday 19 December **4th Sunday of Advent**	*P* Isaiah 7.10–16 Psalm 80.1–8, 18–20 [or 80.1–8] Romans 1.1–7 Matthew 1.18–end	Psalm 144 Micah 5.2–5a Luke 1.26–38	Psalms 113 [126] 1 Samuel 1.1–20 Revelation 22.6–end *HC* Luke 1.39–45
	From 20 December until the Epiphany the seasonal psalmody must be used at Morning and Evening Prayer.		
	Holy Communion	**Morning Prayer**	**Evening Prayer**
Monday 20 December	*P* Isaiah 7.10–14 Psalm 24.1–6 Luke 1.26–38	Psalms **46**, 95 Isaiah 52.13–end of 53 2 Peter 1.1–15	Psalms **4**, 9 Malachi 1.1, 6–end Matthew 19.1–12
Tuesday 21 December	*P* Zephaniah 3.14–18 Psalm 33.1–4, 11–12, 20–end Luke 1.39–45	Psalms 121, 122, 123 Isaiah 54 2 Peter 1.16–2.3	Psalms 80, **84** Malachi 2.1–16 Matthew 19.13–15
Wednesday 22 December	*P* 1 Samuel 1.24–end Psalm 113 Luke 1.46–56	Psalms **124**, 125, 126, 127 Isaiah 55 2 Peter 2.4–end	Psalms 24, **48** Malachi 2.17–3.12 Matthew 19.16–end
Thursday 23 December	*P* Malachi 3.1–4, 4.5–end Psalm 25.3–9 Luke 1.57–66	Psalms 128, 129, **130**, 131 Isaiah 56.1–8 2 Peter 3	Psalm **89.1–37** Malachi 3.13–end of 4 Matthew 23.1–12
	Principal Service	**Morning Prayer**	**Evening Prayer**
Friday 24 December **Christmas Eve**	*P* *Morning Eucharist only:* 2 Samuel 7.1–5, 8–11, 16 Psalm 89.2, 19–27 Acts 13.16–26 Luke 1.67–79	Psalms 45, 113 Isaiah 63.1–6 2 John	Psalm 85 Zechariah 2 Revelation 1.1–8
Saturday 25 December **Christmas Day**	*Gold or W* Any of the following three sets of Principal Service readings may be used on the evening of Christmas Eve and on Christmas Day. Set III should be used at some point during the celebration. Set I Set II Set III Isaiah 9.2–7 Isaiah 62.6–end Isaiah 52.7–10 Psalm 96 Psalm 97 Psalm 98 Titus 2.11–14 Titus 3.4–7 Hebrews 1.1–4 [5–12] Luke 2.1–14 [15–20] Luke 2.[1–7] 8–20 John 1.1–14	*MP* Psalms **110**, 117 Isaiah 62.1–5 Matthew 1.18–end	*EP* Psalm 8 Isaiah 65.17–25 Philippians 2.5–11 or Luke 2.1–20 *if it has not been used at the principal service of the day*

13

Stephen / Christmas 1

	Principal Service	3rd Service	2nd Service
Sunday 26 December R Stephen, deacon, first martyr	2 Chronicles 24.20–22 *or* Acts 7.51–end Psalm 119.161–168 Acts 7.51–end *or* Galatians 2.16b–20 Matthew 10.17–22	*MP* Psalms **13**, 31.1–8, 150 Jeremiah 26.12–15 Acts 6	*EP* Psalms 57, **86** Genesis 4.1–10 Matthew 23.34–end
Or: **Sunday 26 December** W **1st Sunday of Christmas**	Isaiah 63.7–9 Psalm 148 [*or* 148.7–end] Hebrews 2.10–end Matthew 2.13–end	Psalm 105.1–11 Isaiah 35.1–6 Galatians 3.23–end	Psalm 132 Isaiah 49.7–13 Philippians 2.1–11 *HC* Luke 2.41–52
Monday 27 December W John, Apostle and Evangelist	Exodus 33.7–11a Psalm 117 1 John 1 John 21.19b–end	*MP* Psalms **21**, 147.13–end Exodus 33.12–end 1 John 2.1–11	*EP* Psalm **97** Isaiah 6.1–8 1 John 5.1–12
Tuesday 28 December R The Holy Innocents	Jeremiah 31.15–17 Psalm 124 1 Corinthians 1.26–29 Matthew 2.13–18	*MP* Psalms **36**, 146 Baruch 4.21–27 *or* Genesis 37.13–20 Matthew 18.1–10	*EP* Psalms 123, **128** Isaiah 49.14–25 Mark 10.13–16
	Holy Communion	**Morning Prayer**	**Evening Prayer**
Wednesday 29 December Wr Thomas Becket, archbishop, martyr, 1170 (see p. 72)	1 John 2.3–11 Psalm 96.1–4 Luke 2.22–35	Psalms **19**, 20 Isaiah 57.15–end John 1.1–18	Psalms 131, **132** Jonah 1 Colossians 1.1–14
Or, if Stephen has not been celebrated on 26 December:			
	Principal Service	**3rd Service**	**2nd Service**
Wednesday 29 December R Stephen, deacon, first martyr	2 Chronicles 24.20–22 *or* Acts 7.51–end Psalm 119.161–168 Acts 7.51–end *or* Galatians 2.16b–20 Matthew 10.17–22	*MP* Psalms **13**, 31.1–8, 150 Jeremiah 26.12–15 Acts 6	*EP* Psalms 57, **86** Genesis 4.1–10 Matthew 23.34–end

		Holy Communion	Morning Prayer	Evening Prayer
Thursday 30 December	W	1 John 2.12–17 Psalm 96.7–10 Luke 2.36–40	Psalms 111, 112, **113** Isaiah 59.1–15a John 1.19–28	Psalms **65**, 84 Jonah 2 Colossians 1.15–23
Friday 31 December *John Wyclif, reformer, 1384*	W	1 John 2.18–21 Psalm 96.1, 11–end John 1.1–18	Psalm **102** Isaiah 59.15b–end John 1.29–34	Psalms **90**, 148 Jonah 3–4 Colossians 1.24—2.7 *or:* 1st EP of the Naming and Circumcision of Jesus: Psalm 148; Jeremiah 23.1–6; Colossians 2.8–15

		Principal Service	3rd Service	2nd Service
Saturday 1 January Naming and Circumcision of Jesus	W	Numbers 6.22–end Psalm 8 Galatians 4.4–7 Luke 2.15–21	*MP* Psalms **103**, 150 Genesis 17.1–13 Romans 2.17–end	*EP* Psalm **115** Deuteronomy 30. [1–10] 11–end Acts 3.1–16 *or, if the Epiphany is celebrated on Sunday 2 January:* **1st EP of the Epiphany:** Psalms 96, **97**; Isaiah 49.1–13; John 4.7–26

15

Christmas 2 / Epiphany

If the Epiphany is celebrated on Thursday 6 January:

Day		Principal Service	3rd Service	2nd Service
Sunday 2 January 2nd Sunday of Christmas	W	Jeremiah 31.7–14￼ Psalm 147.13–end￼ Ecclesiasticus 24.1–12￼ *Canticle:* Wisdom of Solomon 10.15–end￼ Ephesians 1.3–14￼ John 1.[1–9] 10–18	Psalm 87￼ Jeremiah 31.15–17￼ 2 Corinthians 1.3–12	Psalm 135 [or 135.1–14]￼ Isaiah 41.21—42.4￼ Colossians 1.1–14￼ HC Matthew 2.13–23

Day		Holy Communion	Morning Prayer	Evening Prayer
Monday 3 January	W	1 John 2.29—3.6￼ Psalm 98.2–7￼ John 1.29–34	Psalms 127, 128, 131￼ Isaiah 60.13–end￼ John 1.43–end	Psalms **2**, 110￼ Ruth 2￼ Colossians 3.1–11
Tuesday 4 January	W	1 John 3.7–10￼ Psalm 98.1, 8–end￼ John 1.35–42	Psalm **89.1–37**￼ Isaiah 61￼ John 2.1–12	Psalms 85, **87**￼ Ruth 3￼ Colossians 3.12—4.1
Wednesday 5 January	W	1 John 3.11–21￼ Psalm 100￼ John 1.43–end	Psalms 8, **48**￼ Isaiah 62￼ John 2.13–end	**1st EP of the Epiphany:** Psalms 96, **97**￼ Isaiah 49.1–13￼ John 4.7–26

Day		Principal Service	3rd Service	2nd Service
Thursday 6 January Epiphany	Gold or W	Isaiah 60.1–6￼ Psalm 72.[1–9] 10–15￼ Ephesians 3.1–12￼ Matthew 2.1–12	MP Psalms **132**, 113￼ Jeremiah 31.7–14￼ John 1.29–34	EP Psalms **98**, 100￼ Baruch 4.36—end of 5 or Isaiah 60.1–9￼ John 2.1–11

Day		Holy Communion	Morning Prayer	Evening Prayer
Friday 7 January	W	1 John 3.22—4.6￼ Psalm 2.7–end￼ Matthew 4.12–17, 23–end	Psalms **99**, 147.1–12 or 55￼ Isaiah 63.7–end￼ 1 John 3	Psalms 118 or 69￼ Baruch 1.15—2.10 or Jeremiah 23.1–8￼ Matthew 20.1–16
Saturday 8 January	W	1 John 4.7–10￼ Psalm 72.1–8￼ Mark 6.34–44	Psalms **46**, 147.13–end or **76**, 79￼ Isaiah 64￼ 1 John 4.7–end	Psalms **145** or 81, **84**￼ Baruch 2.11–end or Jeremiah 30.1–17￼ Matthew 20.17–28￼ *or:* 1st EP of the Baptism of Christ: Psalm 36; Isaiah 61; Titus 2.11–14; 3.4–7

16

If the Epiphany is celebrated on Sunday 2 January:

		Principal Service	3rd Service	2nd Service
		Holy Communion	**Morning Prayer**	**Evening Prayer**
Sunday **2 January** Epiphany	Gold or W	Isaiah 60.1-6 Psalm 72.[1-9] 10-15 Ephesians 3.1-12 Matthew 2.1-12	MP Psalms **132**, 113 Jeremiah 31.7-14 John 1.29-34	EP Psalms **98**, 100 Baruch 4.36—end of 5 or Isaiah 60.1-9 John 2.1-11
Monday **3 January**	W	1 John 3.22—4.6 Psalm 2.7-end Matthew 4.12-17, 23-end	Psalms 127, 128, 131 or 71 Isaiah 60.1-12 John 1.35-42	Psalms **2**, 110 or **72**, 75 Ruth 1 Colossians 2.8-end
Tuesday **4 January**	W	1 John 4.7-10 Psalm 72.1-8 Mark 6.34-44	Psalm **89**.1-37 or 73 Isaiah 60.13-end John 1.43-end	Psalms 85, **87** or 74 Ruth 2 Colossians 3.1-11
Wednesday **5 January**	W	1 John 4.11-18 Psalm 72.1, 10-13 Mark 6.45-52	Psalms 8, **48** or 77 Isaiah 61 John 2.1-12	Psalms 96, **97** or 119.81-104 Ruth 3 Colossians 3.12—4.1
Thursday **6 January**	W	1 John 4.19—5.4 Psalm 72.1, 17-end Luke 4.14-22	Psalm **18**.1-30 or **78**.1-39* Isaiah 62 John 2.13-end	Psalms 45, **46** or **78**.40-end* Ruth 4.1-17 Colossians 4.2-end
Friday **7 January**	W	1 John 5.5-13 Psalm 147.13-end Luke 5.12-16	Psalms **99**, 147.1-12 or **55** Isaiah 63.7-end 1 John 3	Psalm 118 or 69 Baruch 1.15—2.10 or Jeremiah 23.1-8 Matthew 20.1-16
Saturday **8 January**	W	1 John 5.14-end Psalm 149.1-5 John 3.22-30	Psalms **46**, 147.13-end or **76**, 79 Isaiah 64 1 John 4.7-end	Psalms **145** or 81, 84 Baruch 2.11-end or Jeremiah 30.1-17 Matthew 20.17-28 or: 1st EP of the Baptism of Christ: Psalm 36; Isaiah 61; Titus 2.11-14; 3.4-7

Baptism of Christ / Epiphany 1

		Principal Service	3rd Service	2nd Service
		Holy Communion	Morning Prayer	Evening Prayer
Sunday **9 January** The Baptism of Christ *1st Sunday of Epiphany*	*Gold or W*	Isaiah 42.1–9 Psalm 29 Acts 10.34–43 Matthew 3.13–end	Psalm 89.19–29 Exodus 14.15–22 1 John 5.6–9	Psalms 46, 47 Joshua 3.1–8, 14–end Hebrews 1.1–12 HC Luke 3.15–22
Monday **10 January** *William Laud, archbishop, 1645* DEL week 1	W	Hebrews 1.1–6 Psalm 97.1–2, 6–10 Mark 1.14–20	Psalms **2**, 110 or **80**, 82 Amos 1 1 Corinthians 1.1–17	Psalms **34**, 36 or **85**, 86 Genesis 1.1–19 Matthew 21.1–17
Tuesday **11 January** *Mary Slessor, missionary, 1915*	W	Hebrews 2.5–12 Psalm 8 Mark 1.21–28	Psalms 8, **9** or 87, **89.1–18** Amos 2 1 Corinthians 1.18–end	Psalms **45**, 46 or **89.19–end** Genesis 1.20—2.3 Matthew 21.18–32
Wednesday **12 January** *Aelred, abbot, 1167 (see p.75)* *Benedict Biscop, scholar, 689*	W	Hebrews 2.14–end Psalm 105.1–9 Mark 1.29–39	Psalms 19, **20** or **119.105–128** Amos 3 1 Corinthians 2	Psalms 47, **48** or **91**, 93 Genesis 2.4–end Matthew 21.33–end
Thursday **13 January** *Hilary, bishop, teacher of the faith, 367 (see p.73)* *Kentigern (Mungo), missionary bishop, 603* *George Fox, founder of the Society of Friends (Quakers), 1691*	W	Hebrews 3.7–14 Psalm 95.1, 8–end Mark 1.40–end	Psalms **21**, 24 or 90, **92** Amos 4 1 Corinthians 3	Psalms **61**, 65 or **94** Genesis 3 Matthew 22.1–14
Friday **14 January**	W	Hebrews 4.1–5, 11 Psalm 78.3–8 Mark 2.1–12	Psalms 67, **72** or 88 (95) Amos 5.1–17 1 Corinthians 4	Psalm **68** or **102** Genesis 4.1–16, 25–26 Matthew 22.15–33
Saturday **15 January**	W	Hebrews 4.12–end Psalm 19.7–end Mark 2.13–17	Psalms 29, **33** or 96, **97**, 100 Amos 5.18–end 1 Corinthians 5	Psalms 84, **85** or **104** Genesis 6.1–10 Matthew 22.34–end

		Principal Service	3rd Service	2nd Service
Sunday	**16 January** W 2nd Sunday of Epiphany	Isaiah 49.1–7 Psalm 40.1–12 1 Corinthians 1.1–9 John 1.29–42	Psalm 145.1–12 Jeremiah 1.4–10 Mark 1.14–20	Psalm 96 Ezekiel 2.1—3.4 Galatians 1.11–end *HC* John 1.43–end
		Holy Communion	**Morning Prayer**	**Evening Prayer**
Monday	**17 January** W *Antony of Egypt, hermit, abbot, 356 (see p. 75)* *Charles Gore, bishop, founder of the Community of the Resurrection, 1932* DEL week 2	Hebrews 5.1–10 Psalm 110.1–4 Mark 2.18–22	Psalms 145, **146** or **98**, 99, 101 Amos 6 1 Corinthians 6.1–11	Psalm 71 or **105*** (or 103) Genesis 6.11—7.10 Matthew 24.1–14
Tuesday	**18 January** W Week of Prayer for Christian Unity: 18–25 January	Hebrews 6.10–end Psalm 111 Mark 2.23–end	Psalms **132**, 147.1–12 or **106*** (or 103) Amos 7 1 Corinthians 6.12–end	Psalms **89**.1–37 or **107*** Genesis 7.11–end Matthew 24.15–28
Wednesday	**19 January** W *Wulfstan, bishop, 1095 (see p. 74)*	Hebrews 7.1–3, 15–17 Psalm 110.1–4 Mark 3.1–6	Psalms **81**, 147.13–end or 110, **111**, 112 Amos 8 1 Corinthians 7.1–24	Psalms **97**, 98 or **119**.129–152 Genesis 8.1–14 Matthew 24.29–end
Thursday	**20 January** W *Richard Rolle, spiritual writer, 1349*	Hebrews 7.25—8.6 Psalm 40.7–10, 17–end Mark 3.7–12	Psalms **76**, 148 or 113, **115** Amos 9 1 Corinthians 7.25–end	Psalms 99, **100**, **111** or 114, **116**, 117 Genesis 8.15—9.7 Matthew 25.1–13
Friday	**21 January** Wr *Agnes, child martyr, 304 (see p. 72)*	Hebrews 8.6–end Psalm 85.7–end Mark 3.13–19	Psalms 27, **149** or **139** Hosea 1.1—2.1 1 Corinthians 8	Psalms **73** or **130**, 131, 137 Genesis 9.8–19 Matthew 25.14–30
Saturday	**22 January** W *Vincent of Saragossa, deacon, martyr, 304*	Hebrews 9.2–3, 11–14 Psalm 47.1–8 Mark 3.20–21	Psalms **122**, 128, 150 or 120, **121**, 122 Hosea 2.2–17 1 Corinthians 9.1–14	Psalms **61**, 66 or **118** Genesis 11.1–9 Matthew 25.31–end

Epiphany 3

		Principal Service	3rd Service	2nd Service
Sunday	**23 January** W **3rd Sunday of Epiphany**	Isaiah 9.1–4 Psalm 27.1, 4–12 [or 27.1–11] 1 Corinthians 1.10–18 Matthew 4.12–23	Psalm 113 Amos 3.1–8 1 John 1.1–4	Psalm 33 [or 33.1–12] Ecclesiastes 3.1–11 1 Peter 1.3–12 HC Luke 4.14–21

		Holy Communion	Morning Prayer	Evening Prayer
Monday	**24 January** W Francis de Sales, bishop, teacher of the faith, 1622 (see p. 73) DEL week 3	Hebrews 9.15, 24–end Psalm 98.1–7 Mark 3.22–30	Psalms 40, **108** or 123, 124, 125, **126** Hosea 2.18–end of 3 1 Corinthians 9.15–end	Psalms 138, 144 or **127**, 128, 129 Genesis 11.27—12.9 Matthew 26.1–16 or: 1st EP of the Conversion of Paul: Psalm 149; Isaiah 49.1–13; Acts 22.3–16

		Principal Service	3rd Service	2nd Service
Tuesday	**25 January** W Conversion of Paul	Jeremiah 1.4–10 or Acts 9.1–22 Psalm 67 Acts 9.1–22 or Galatians 1.11–16a Matthew 19.27–end	MP Psalms 66, 147.13–end Ezekiel 3.22–end Philippians 3.1–14	EP Psalm 119.41–56 Ecclesiasticus 39.1–10 or Isaiah 56.1–8 Colossians 1.24—2.7

		Holy Communion	Morning Prayer	Evening Prayer
Wednesday	**26 January** W Timothy and Titus, companions of Paul	Hebrews 10.11–18 Psalm 110.1–4 Mark 4.1–20 *Lesser Festival eucharistic lectionary:* Isaiah 61.1–3a; Psalm 100; 2 Timothy 2.1–8 or Titus 1.1–5; Luke 10.1–9	Psalms **45**, **46** or **119.153–end** Hosea 5.1–7 1 Corinthians 10.14—11.1	Psalms 21, **29** or 136 Genesis 14 Matthew 26.36–46
Thursday	**27 January** W	Hebrews 10.19–25 Psalm 24.1–6 Mark 4.21–25	Psalms **47**, 48 or **143**, 146 Hosea 5.8—6.6 1 Corinthians 11.2–16	Psalms **24**, 33 or **138**, 140, 141 Genesis 15 Matthew 26.47–56
Friday	**28 January** W Thomas Aquinas, priest, philosopher, teacher of the faith, 1274 (see p. 73)	Hebrews 10.32–end Psalm 37.3–6, 40–end Mark 4.26–34	Psalms 61, **65** or 142, 144 Hosea 6.7—7.2 1 Corinthians 11.17–end	Psalms **67**, 77 or 145 Genesis 16 Matthew 26.57–end
Saturday	**29 January** W	Hebrews 11.1–2, 8–19 Canticle: Luke 1.69–73 Mark 4.35–end	Psalm **68** or 147 Hosea 8 1 Corinthians 12.1–11	Psalms 72, 76 or **148**, 149, 150 Genesis 17.1–22 Matthew 27.1–10 *or, if the Presentation is celebrated on Sunday 30 January:* **1st EP of the Presentation:** Psalm 118; 1 Samuel 1.19b–end; Hebrews 4.11—end

Epiphany 4 / Presentation

If the Presentation of Christ in the Temple is celebrated on Wednesday 2 February:

	Principal Service	3rd Service	2nd Service
Sunday 30 January W **4th Sunday of Epiphany**	1 Kings 17.8–16 Psalm 36.5–10 1 Corinthians 1.18–end John 2.1–11	Psalm 71.1–6, 15–17 Haggai 2.1–9 1 Corinthians 3.10–17	Psalm 34 [or 34.1–10] Genesis 28.10–end Philemon 1–16 HC Mark 1.21–28
	Holy Communion	**Morning Prayer**	**Evening Prayer**
Monday 31 January W *John Bosco, priest, founder of the Salesian Teaching Order, 1888* DEL week 4	Hebrews 11.32–end Psalm 31.19–end Mark 5.1–20	Psalms **57**, 96 or 1, 2, 3 Hosea 9 1 Corinthians 12.12–end	Psalms 2, **20** or 4, **7** Genesis 18.1–15 Matthew 27.11–26
	Principal Service	**Morning Prayer**	
Tuesday 1 February W *Brigid, abbess, c.525*	Hebrews 12.1–4 Psalm 22.25b–end Mark 5.21–43	Psalms 93, 97 or **5**, 6 (8) Hosea 10 1 Corinthians 13	**1st EP of the Presentation:** Psalm 118 1 Samuel 1.19b–end Hebrews 4.11–end
	Principal Service	**3rd Service**	**2nd Service**
Wednesday 2 February Gold or W **Presentation of Christ in the Temple** **(Candlemas)**	Malachi 3.1–5 Psalm 24. [1–6] 7–end Hebrews 2.14–end Luke 2.22–40	MP Psalms **48**, 146 Exodus 13.1–16 Romans 12.1–5	EP Psalms 122, **132** Haggai 2.1–9 John 2.18–22
	Holy Communion	**Morning Prayer**	**Evening Prayer**
Thursday 3 February Gw *Anskar, archbishop, missionary, 865* *(see p. 75)* Ordinary Time starts today. The Collect of 5 before Lent is used.	Hebrews 12.18–19, 21–24 Psalm 48.1–3, 8–10 Mark 6.7–13	Psalms 14, **15**, 16 Hosea 11.12–end of 12 1 Corinthians 14.20–end	Psalm 18* Genesis 21.1–21 Matthew 27.57–end
	Principal Service	**Morning Prayer**	**Evening Prayer**
Friday 4 February G *Gilbert, founder of the Gilbertine Order, 1189*	Hebrews 13.1–8 Psalm 27.1–6, 9–12 Mark 6.14–29	Psalms 17, **19** Hosea 13.1–14 1 Corinthians 16.1–9	Psalm 22 Genesis 22.1–19 Matthew 28.1–15
Saturday 5 February G	Hebrews 13.15–17, 20–21 Psalm 23 Mark 6.30–34	Psalms 20, 21, **23** Hosea 14 1 Corinthians 16.10–end	Psalms **24**, 25 Genesis 23 Matthew 28.16–end

Presentation

If the Presentation of Christ in the Temple is celebrated on Sunday 30 January:

	Principal Service	3rd Service	2nd Service
Sunday *Gold or W* **30 January** Presentation of Christ in the Temple *(if transferred from 2 February)* (Candlemas)	Malachi 3.1–5 Psalm 24. [1–6] 7–end Hebrews 2.14–end Luke 2.22–40	*MP* Psalms **48**, 146 Exodus 13.1–16 Romans 12.1–5	*EP* Psalms 122, **132** Haggai 2.1–9 John 2.18–22
	Holy Communion	**Morning Prayer**	**Evening Prayer**
Monday *G* **31 January** *John Bosco, priest, founder of the Salesian Teaching Order, 1888* Ordinary Time starts today if the Presentation was celebrated on 30 January. The Collect of 5 before Lent is used. DEL week 4	Hebrews 11.32–end Psalm 31.19–end Mark 5.1–20	Psalms **1**, 2, 3 Hosea 9 1 Corinthians 12.12–end	Psalms 4, 7 Genesis 18.1–15 Matthew 27.11–26
Tuesday 1 February *G* *Brigid, abbess, c.525*	Hebrews 12.1–4 Psalm 22.25b–end Mark 5.21–43	Psalms **5**, 6 (8) Hosea 10 1 Corinthians 13	Psalms **9**, 10* Genesis 18.16–end Matthew 27.27–44
Wednesday 2 February *G*	Hebrews 12.4–7, 11–15 Psalm 103.1–2, 13–18 Mark 6.1–6	Psalm **119.1–32** Hosea 11.1–11 1 Corinthians 14.1–19	Psalms 11, 12, 13 Genesis 19.1–3, 12–29 Matthew 27.45–56
Thursday 3 February *Gw* Anskar, archbishop, missionary, 865 *(see p. 75)*	Hebrews 12.18–19, 21–24 Psalm 48.1–3, 8–10 Mark 6.7–13	Psalms 14, **15**, 16 Hosea 11.12–end of 12 1 Corinthians 14.20–end	Psalm **18*** Genesis 21.1–21 Matthew 27.57–end
Friday 4 February *G* *Gilbert, founder of the Gilbertine Order, 1189*	Hebrews 13.1–8 Psalm 27.1–6, 9–12 Mark 6.14–29	Psalms 17, **19** Hosea 13.1–14 1 Corinthians 16.1–9	Psalm **22** Genesis 22.1–19 Matthew 28.1–15
Saturday 5 February *G*	Hebrews 13.15–17, 20–21 Psalm 23 Mark 6.30–34	Psalms 20, 21, **23** Hosea 14 1 Corinthians 16.10–end	Psalms **24**, 25 Genesis 23 Matthew 28.16–end

		Principal Service	3rd Service	2nd Service
Sunday	**6 February** G **5th Sunday before Lent** *Accession of Queen Elizabeth II, 1952* (see p. 78) Proper 1	Isaiah 58.1–9a [9b–12] Psalm 112.1–9 [–end] 1 Corinthians 2.1–12 [13–end] Matthew 5.13–20	Psalms 5, 6 Jeremiah 26.1–16 Acts 3.1–10	Psalms [1, 3] 4 Amos 2.4–end Ephesians 4.17–end HC Mark 1.29–39
		Holy Communion	Morning Prayer	Evening Prayer
Monday	**7 February** G DEL week 5	Genesis 1.1–19 Psalm 104.1,2,6–13, 26 Mark 6.53–end	Psalms 27, **30** 1 Chronicles 10.1—11.9 John 13.1–11	Psalms 26, **28**, **29** Exodus 22.21–27, 23.1–17 Philippians 1.1–11
Tuesday	**8 February** G	Genesis 1.20—2.4a Psalm 8 Mark 7.1–13	Psalms 32, **36** 1 Chronicles 13 John 13.12–20	Psalm **33** Exodus 29.38—30.16 Philippians 1.12–end
Wednesday	**9 February** G	Genesis 2.4b–9, 15–17 Psalm 104.11–12, 29–32 Mark 7.14–23	Psalm **34** 1 Chronicles 15.1—16.3 John 13.21–30	Psalm 119.**33–56** Leviticus 8 Philippians 2.1–13
Thursday	**10 February** G *Scholastica, abbess, c.543*	Genesis 2.18–end Psalm 128 Mark 7.24–30	Psalm **37*** 1 Chronicles 17 John 13.31–end	Psalms 39, **40** Leviticus 9 Philippians 2.14–end
Friday	**11 February** G	Genesis 3.1–8 Psalm 32.1–8 Mark 7.31–end	Psalm **31** 1 Chronicles 21.1—22.1 John 14.1–14	Psalm **35** Leviticus 16.2–24 Philippians 3.1—4.1
Saturday	**12 February** G	Genesis 3.9–end Psalm 90.1–12 Mark 8.1–10	Psalms 41, **42**, **43** 1 Chronicles 22.2–end John 14.15–end	Psalms 45, **46** Leviticus 17 Philippians 4.2–end

	Principal Service	3rd Service	2nd Service
Sunday **13 February** G **4th Sunday before Lent** Proper 2	Deuteronomy 30.15–end or Ecclesiasticus 15.15–end Psalm 119.1–8 1 Corinthians 3.1–9 Matthew 5.21–37	Psalm 10 Jeremiah 30.1–3, 10–22 Acts 6	Psalms [7] 13 Amos 3.1–8 Ephesians 5.1–17 HC Mark 1.40–end
	Holy Communion	**Morning Prayer**	**Evening Prayer**
Monday **14 February** Gw Cyril and Methodius, missionaries, 869 and 885 (see p. 75) *Valentine, martyr at Rome, c.269* DEL week 6	Genesis 4.1–15, 25 Psalm 50.1, 8, 16–end Mark 8.11–13	Psalm 44 1 Chronicles 28.1–10 John 15.1–11	Psalms **47**, 49 Leviticus 19.1–18, 30–end 1 Timothy 1.1–17
Tuesday **15 February** G *Sigfrid, bishop, 1045* *Thomas Bray, priest, founder of SPCK and SPG, 1730*	Genesis 6.5–8; 7.1–5, 10 Psalm 29 Mark 8.14–21	Psalms **48**, 52 1 Chronicles 28.11–end John 15.12–17	Psalm **50** Leviticus 23.1–22 1 Timothy 1.18–end of 2
Wednesday **16 February** G	Genesis 8.6–13, 20–end Psalm 116.10–end Mark 8.22–26	Psalm 1**19**.57–80 1 Chronicles 29.1–9 John 15.18–end	Psalms **59**, 60 (67) Leviticus 23.23–end 1 Timothy 3
Thursday **17 February** Gr Janani Luwum, archbishop, martyr, 1977 (see p. 72)	Genesis 9.1–13 Psalm 102.16–23 Mark 8.27–33	Psalms 56, **57** (63*) 1 Chronicles 29.10–20 John 16.1–15	Psalms 61, **62**, 64 Leviticus 24.1–9 1 Timothy 4
Friday **18 February** G	Genesis 11.1–9 Psalm 33.10–15 Mark 8.34—9.1	Psalms 51, 54 1 Chronicles 29.21–end John 16.16–22	Psalm 38 Leviticus 25.1–24 1 Timothy 5.1–16
Saturday **19 February** G	Hebrews 11.1–7 Psalm 145.1–10 Mark 9.2–13	Psalm 68 2 Chronicles 1.1–13 John 16.23–end	Psalms 65, **66** Numbers 6.1–5, 21–end 1 Timothy 5.17–end

		Principal Service	3rd Service	2nd Service
Sunday				
20 February 3rd Sunday before Lent Proper 3	G	Leviticus 19.1–2, 9–18 Psalm 119.33–40 1 Corinthians 3.10–11, 16–end Matthew 5.38–end	Psalms 21, 23 Jeremiah 33.1–11 Acts 8.4–25	Psalm 18.1–20 or 18.21–30 Amos 9.5–end Ephesians 6.1–20 HC Mark 2.1–12
		Holy Communion	Morning Prayer	Evening Prayer
Monday 21 February DEL week 7	G	Ecclesiasticus 1.1–10 or James 1.1–11 Psalm 93 or 119.65–72 Mark 9.14–29	Psalm 71 2 Chronicles 2.1–16 John 17.1–5	Psalms 72, 75 Genesis 24.1–28 1 Timothy 6.1–10
Tuesday 22 February	G	Ecclesiasticus 2.1–11 or James 1.12–18 Psalm 37.3–6, 27–28 or 94.12–18 Mark 9.30–37	Psalm 73 2 Chronicles 3 John 17.6–19	Psalm 74 Genesis 24.29–end 1 Timothy 6.11–end
Wednesday 23 February Polycarp, bishop, martyr, c.155 (see p.72)	Gr	Ecclesiasticus 4.11–19 or James 1.19–end Psalm 119.161–168 or 15 Mark 9.38–40	Psalm 77 2 Chronicles 5 John 17.20–end	Psalms 119.81–104 Genesis 25.7–11, 19–end 2 Timothy 1.1–14
Thursday 24 February	G	Ecclesiasticus 5.1–8 or James 2.1–9 Psalm 1 or 34.1–7 Mark 9.41–end	Psalm 78.1–39* 2 Chronicles 6.1–21 John 18.1–11	Psalm 78.40–end* Genesis 26.34–27.40 2 Timothy 1.15—2.13
Friday 25 February	G	Ecclesiasticus 6.5–17 or James 2.14–24, 26 Psalm 119.19–24 or 112 Mark 10.1–12	Psalm 55 2 Chronicles 6.22–end John 18.12–27	Psalm 69 Genesis 27.41—end of 28 2 Timothy 2.14–end
Saturday 26 February	G	Ecclesiasticus 17.1–15 or James 3.1–10 Psalm 103.13–18 or 12.1–7 Mark 10.13–16	Psalms 76, 79 2 Chronicles 7 John 18.28–end	Psalms 81, 84 Genesis 29.1–30 2 Timothy 3

		Principal Service	3rd Service	2nd Service
Sunday	**27 February** G **2nd Sunday before Lent**	Genesis 1.1—2.3 Psalm 136 or Psalm 136.1—9, 23—end Romans 8.18—25 Matthew 6.25—end	Psalms 100, 150 Job 38.1—21 Colossians 1.15—20	Psalm 148 Proverbs 8.1, 22—31 Revelation 4 HC Luke 12.16—31
		Holy Communion	**Morning Prayer**	**Evening Prayer**
Monday	**28 February** G DEL week 8	Ecclesiasticus 17.24—29 or James 3.13—end Psalm 32.1—8 or 19.7—end Mark 10.17—27	Psalms 80, 82 2 Chronicles 9.1—12 John 19.1—16	Psalms 85, 86 Genesis 29.31—30.24 2 Timothy 4.1—8
Tuesday	**1 March** Gw David, bishop, patron of Wales, c. 601 (see p. 74)	Ecclesiasticus 35.1—12 or James 4.1—10 Psalm 50.1—6 or 55.7—9, 24 Mark 10.28—31	Psalms 87, **89.1—18** 2 Chronicles 10.1—11.4 John 19.17—30	Psalm **89.19—end** Genesis 31.1—24 2 Timothy 4.9—end
Wednesday	**2 March** Gw Chad, bishop, missionary, 672 (see p. 75)	Ecclesiasticus 36.1—2, 4—5, 10—17 or James 4.13—end Psalm 79.8—9, 12, 14 or 49.1—2, 5—10 Mark 10.32—45	Psalm 119.**105—128** 2 Chronicles 12 John 19.31—end	Psalms 91, 93 Genesis 31.25—32.2 Titus 1
Thursday	**3 March** G	Ecclesiasticus 42.15—end or James 5.1—6 Psalm 33.1—9 or 49.12—20 Mark 10.46—end	Psalms 90, **92** 2 Chronicles 13.1—14.1 John 20.1—10	Psalm **94** Genesis 32.3—30 Titus 2
Friday	**4 March** G	Ecclesiasticus 44.1, 9—13 or James 5.9—12 Psalm 149.1—5 or 103.1—4, 8—13 Mark 11.11—26	Psalms 88 (95) 2 Chronicles 14.2—end John 20.11—18	Psalm 102 Genesis 33.1—17 Titus 3
Saturday	**5 March** G	Ecclesiasticus 51.12—20 or James 5.13—end Psalm 19.7—end or 141.1—4 Mark 11.27—end	Psalms 96, **97**, 100 2 Chronicles 15.1—15 John 20.19—end	Psalm 104 Genesis 35 Philemon

		Principal Service	3rd Service	2nd Service
Sunday 6 March **Sunday next before Lent**	G	Exodus 24.12–end Psalm 2 or Psalm 99 2 Peter 1.16–end Matthew 17.1–9	Psalm 72 Exodus 34.29–end 2 Corinthians 4.3–6	Psalm 84 Ecclesiasticus 48.1–10 or 2 Kings 2.1–12 Matthew 17.9–23 (or 1–23)
		Holy Communion	*Morning Prayer*	*Evening Prayer*
Monday 7 March Perpetua, Felicity and companions, martyrs, 203 (see p. 72) DEL week 9	Gr	Tobit 1.1–2, 2.1–8 or 1 Peter 1.3–9 Psalm 15 or 111 Mark 12.1–12	Psalm **98**, 99, 101 Jeremiah 1 John 3.1–21	Psalm **105*** (or 103) Genesis 37.1–11 Galatians 1
Tuesday 8 March Edward King, bishop, 1910 (see p. 74) *Felix, bishop, 647* *Geoffrey Studdert Kennedy, priest, poet, 1929*	Gw	Tobit 2.9–end or 1 Peter 1.10–16 Psalm 112 or 98.1–5 Mark 12.13–17	Psalm **106*** (or 103) Jeremiah 2.1–13 John 3.22–end	Psalm **107*** Genesis 37.12–end Galatians 2.1–10
		Principal Service	*3rd Service*	*2nd Service*
Wednesday 9 March **Ash Wednesday**	P(La)	Joel 2.1–2, 12–17 or Isaiah 58.1–12 Psalm 51.1–18 2 Corinthians 5.20b–6.10 Matthew 6.1–6, 16–21 or John 8.1–11	MP Psalm 38 Daniel 9.3–6, 17–19 1 Timothy 6.6–19	EP Psalm **51** or 102 [or 102.1–18] Isaiah 1.10–18 Luke 15.11–end
		Holy Communion	*Morning Prayer*	*Evening Prayer*
Thursday 10 March	P(La)	Deuteronomy 30.15–end Psalm 1 Luke 9.22–25	Psalms **77** or 113, **115** Jeremiah 2.14–32 John 4.1–26	Psalms **74** or 114, **116**, 117 Genesis 39 Galatians 2.11–end
Friday 11 March	P(La)	Isaiah 58.1–9a Psalm 51.1–5, 17–18 Matthew 9.14–15	Psalms **3**, 7 or **139** Jeremiah 3.6–22 John 4.27–42	Psalms 31 or **130**, 131, 137 Genesis 40 Galatians 3.1–14
Saturday 12 March	P(La)	Isaiah 58.9b–end Psalm 86.1–7 Luke 5.27–32	Psalms 71 or 120, **121**, 122 Jeremiah 4.1–18 John 4.43–end	Psalm 73 or 118 Genesis 41.1–24 Galatians 3.15–22

Lent 1

		Principal Service	3rd Service	2nd Service
Sunday 13 March 1st Sunday of Lent	P(La)	Genesis 2.15–17;3.1–7 Psalm 32 Romans 5.12–19 Matthew 4.1–11	Psalm 119.1–16 Jeremiah 18.1–11 Luke 18.9–14	Psalm 50.1–15 Deuteronomy 6.4–9,16–end Luke 15.1–10

		Holy Communion	Morning Prayer	Evening Prayer
Monday 14 March	P(La)	Leviticus 19.1–2,11–18 Psalm 19.7–end Matthew 25.31–end	Psalms 10,11 or 123,124,125,**126** Jeremiah 4.19–end John 5.1–18	Psalms 12,**13**,14 or **127**,128,129 Genesis 41.25–45 Galatians 3.23—4.7
Tuesday 15 March	P(La)	Isaiah 55.10–11 Psalm 34.4–6,21–22 Matthew 6.7–15	Psalms **44** or **132**,133 Jeremiah 5.1–19 John 5.19–29	Psalms 46,**49** or (134), **135** Genesis 41.46—42.5 Galatians 4.8–20
Wednesday 16 March Ember Day	P(La)	Jonah 3 Psalm 51.1–5,17–18 Luke 11.29–32	Psalms **6**,17 or **119.153–end** Jeremiah 5.20–end John 5.30–end	Psalms 9,**28** or **136** Genesis 42.6–17 Galatians 4.21—5.1
Thursday 17 March Patrick, bishop, missionary, patron of Ireland, c.460 (see p.75)	P(La)w	Esther 14.1–5, 12–14 or Isaiah 55.6–9 Psalm 138 Matthew 7.7–12	Psalms **42**,43 or **143**,146 Jeremiah 6.9–21 John 6.1–15	Psalms 137, 138, **142** or **138**, 140, 141 Genesis 42.18–28 Galatians 5.2–15
Friday 18 March Cyril, bishop, teacher of the faith, 386 Ember Day	P(La)	Ezekiel 18.21–28 Psalm 30 Matthew 5.20–26	Psalms **22** or 142,**144** Jeremiah 6.22–end John 6.16–27	Psalms 54,**55** or **145** Genesis 42.29–end Galatians 5.16–end or: 1st EP of Joseph of Nazareth: Psalm 132; Hosea 11.1–9; Luke 2.41–end

		Principal Service	3rd Service	2nd Service
Saturday 19 March Joseph of Nazareth Ember Day	W	2 Samuel 7.4–16 Psalm 89.26–36 Romans 4.13–18 Matthew 1.18–end	MP Psalms 25, 147.1–12 Isaiah 11.1–10 Matthew 13.54–end	EP Psalms 1, 112 Genesis 50.22–end Matthew 2.13–end

	Principal Service	3rd Service	2nd Service
Sunday 20 March P(La) **2nd Sunday of Lent**	Genesis 12.1–4a Psalm 121 Romans 4.1–5, 13–17 John 3.1–17	Psalm 74 Jeremiah 22.1–9 Matthew 8.1–13	Psalm 135 [or 135.1–14] Numbers 21.4–9 Luke 14.27–33
	Holy Communion	**Morning Prayer**	**Evening Prayer**
Monday 21 March P(La)r Thomas Cranmer, archbishop, Reformation martyr, 1556 (see p. 72)	Daniel 9.4–10 Psalm 79.8–9, 12, 14 Luke 6.36–38	Psalms 26, 32 or 1, 2, 3 Jeremiah 7.21–end John 6.41–51	Psalms 70, 74 or 4, 7 Genesis 43.16–end Hebrews 1
Tuesday 22 March P(La)	Isaiah 1.10, 16–20 Psalm 50.8, 16–end Matthew 23.1–12	Psalms 50 or 5, 6 (8) Jeremiah 8.1–15 John 6.52–59	Psalms 52, 53, 54 or 9, 10* Genesis 44.1–17 Hebrews 2.1–9
Wednesday 23 March P(La)	Jeremiah 18.18–20 Psalm 31.4–5, 14–18 Matthew 20.17–28	Psalm 35 or 119.1–32 Jeremiah 8.18–9.11 John 6.60–end	Psalms 3, 5 or 11, 12, 13 Genesis 44.18–end Hebrews 2.10–end
Thursday 24 March P(La) Walter Hilton, mystic, 1396 Oscar Romero, archbishop, martyr, 1980	Jeremiah 17.5–10 Psalm 1 Luke 16.19–end	Psalms 34 or 14, 15, 16 Jeremiah 9.12–24 John 7.1–13	**1st EP of the Annunciation of Our Lord to the BVM:** Psalm 85 Wisdom 9.1–12 or Genesis 3.8–15 Galatians 4.1–5
	Principal Service	**3rd Service**	**2nd Service**
Friday 25 March Gold or W **Annunciation of Our Lord to the Blessed Virgin Mary**	Isaiah 7.10–14 Psalm 40.5–11 Hebrews 10.4–10 Luke 1.26–38	MP Psalms 111, 113 1 Samuel 2.1–10 Romans 5.12–end	EP Psalms 131, 146 Isaiah 52.1–12 Hebrews 2.5–end
	Holy Communion	**Morning Prayer**	**Evening Prayer**
Saturday 26 March P(La) Harriet Monsell, founder of the Community of St John the Baptist, 1883	Micah 7.14–15, 18–20 Psalm 103.1–4, 9–12 Luke 15.1–3, 11–end	Psalms 3, 25 or 20, 21, 23 Jeremiah 10.17–24 John 7.25–36	Psalms 23, 27 or 24, 25 Genesis 46.1–7, 28–end Hebrews 4.1–13

Lent 3

		Principal Service	3rd Service	2nd Service
Sunday	**27 March** P(La) **3rd Sunday of Lent**	Exodus 17.1–7 Psalm 95 Romans 5.1–11 John 4.5–42	Psalm 46 Amos 7.10–end 2 Corinthians 1.1–11	Psalm 40 Joshua 1.1–9 Ephesians 6.10–20 HC John 2.13–22

The following readings may replace those provided for Holy Communion on any day during the Third Week of Lent:
Exodus 17.1–7; Psalm 95.1–7; Psalm 95.1–2, 6–end; John 4.5–42

		Holy Communion	Morning Prayer	Evening Prayer
Monday	**28 March** P(La)	2 Kings 5.1–15 Psalms 42.1–2, 43.1–4 Luke 4.24–30	Psalms **5**, 7 or 27, **30** Jeremiah 11.1–17 John 7.37–52	Psalms 11, **17** or 26, **28**, 29 Genesis 47.1–27 Hebrews 4.14—5.10
Tuesday	**29 March** P(La)	Song of the Three 2, 11–20 or Daniel 2.20–23 Psalm 25.3–10 Matthew 18.21–end	Psalms 6, **9** or 32, **36** Jeremiah 11.18—12.6 John 7.53—8.11	Psalms 61, 62, **64** or 33 Genesis 47.28—end of 48 Hebrews 5.11—6.12
Wednesday	**30 March** P(La)	Deuteronomy 4.1, 5–9 Psalm 147.13–end Matthew 5.17–19	Psalm **38** or 34 Jeremiah 13.1–11 John 8.12–30	Psalms 36, **39** or 119.**33–56** Genesis 49.1–32 Hebrews 6.13–end
Thursday	**31 March** P(La) John Donne, priest, poet, 1631	Jeremiah 7.23–28 Psalm 95.1–2, 6–end Luke 11.14–23	Psalms **56**, 57 or 37* Jeremiah 14 John 8.31–47	Psalms **59**, 60 or 39, **40** Genesis 49.33—end of 50 Hebrews 7.1–10
Friday	**1 April** P(La) Frederick Denison Maurice, priest, teacher of the faith, 1872	Hosea 14 Psalm 81.6–10, 13, 16 Mark 12.28–34	Psalm **22** or 31 Jeremiah 15.10–end John 8.48–end	Psalm **69** or **35** Exodus 1.1–14 Hebrews 7.11–end
Saturday	**2 April** P(La)	Hosea 5.15—6.6 Psalm 51.1–2, 17–end Luke 18.9–14	Psalms **31** or 41, **42**, 43 Jeremiah 16.10—17.4 John 9.1–17	Psalms **116**, 130 or 45, **46** Exodus 1.22—2.10 Hebrews 8

		Principal Service	3rd Service	2nd Service
Sunday	**3 April** P(La) **4th Sunday of Lent**	1 Samuel 16.1–13 Psalm 23 Ephesians 5.8–14 John 9	Psalm 19 Isaiah 43.1–7 Ephesians 2.8–14	Psalm 31.1–16 or 31.1–8 Micah 7 or Prayer of Manasseh James 5 HC John 3.14–21

For Mothering Sunday:
Exodus 2.1–10 or 1 Samuel 1.20–end; Psalm 34.11–20 or 127.1–4;
2 Corinthians 1.3–7 or Colossians 3.12–17; Luke 2.33–35 or John 19.25b–27
If the Principal Service readings have been displaced by Mothering Sunday provisions, they may be used at the Second Service.

		Holy Communion	Morning Prayer	Evening Prayer

The following readings may replace those provided for Holy Communion on any day during the Fourth Week of Lent:
Micah 7.7–9; Psalm 27.1, 9–10, 16–17; John 9

		Holy Communion	Morning Prayer	Evening Prayer
Monday	**4 April** P(La)	Isaiah 65.17–21 Psalm 30.1–5, 8, 11–end John 4.43–end	Psalms 70, 77 or **44** Jeremiah 17.5–18 John 9.18–end	Psalms **25**, 28 or **47**, 49 Exodus 2.11–22 Hebrews 9.1–14
Tuesday	**5 April** P(La)	Ezekiel 47.1–9, 12 Psalm 46.1–8 John 5.1–3, 5–16	Psalms 54, 79 or **48**, 52 Jeremiah 18.1–12 John 10.1–10	Psalms 80, 82 or **50** Exodus 2.23—3.20 Hebrews 9.15–end
Wednesday	**6 April** P(La)	Isaiah 49.8–15 Psalm 145.8–18 John 5.17–30	Psalms 63, **90** or **119.57-80** Jeremiah 18.13–end John 10.11–21	Psalms 52, **91** or 59, 60 (67) Exodus 4.1–23 Hebrews 10.1–18
Thursday	**7 April** P(La)	Exodus 32.7–14 Psalm 106.19–23 John 5.31–end	Psalms 53, **86** or 56, **57** (63*) Jeremiah 19.1–13 John 10.22–end	Psalms **94** or 61, **62**, 64 Exodus 4.27—6.1 Hebrews 10.19–25
Friday	**8 April** P(La)	Wisdom 2.1, 12–22 or Jeremiah 26.8–11 Psalm 34.15–end John 7.1–2, 10, 25–30	Psalms 102 or **51**, 54 Jeremiah 19.14—20.6 John 11.1–16	Psalms 13, **16** or **38** Exodus 6.2–13 Hebrews 10.26–end
Saturday	**9 April** P(La) *Dietrich Bonhoeffer, Lutheran pastor, martyr, 1945*	Jeremiah 11.18–20 Psalm 7.1–2, 8–10 John 7.40–52	Psalm **32** or **68** Jeremiah 20.7–end John 11.17–27	Psalms **140**, 141, 142 or 65, **66** Exodus 7.8–end Hebrews 11.1–16

		Principal Service	3rd Service	2nd Service
Sunday	**10 April** *P(La)* **5th Sunday of Lent** *Passiontide begins*	Ezekiel 37.1–14 Psalm 130 Romans 8.6–11 John 11.1–45	Psalm 86 Jeremiah 31.27–37 John 12.20–33	Psalm 30 Lamentations 3.19–33 Matthew 20.17–end
		Holy Communion	Morning Prayer	Evening Prayer
	The following readings may replace those provided for Holy Communion on any day during the Fifth Week of Lent: 2 Kings 4.18–21, 32–37; Psalm 17.1–8, 16; John 11.1–45			
Monday	**11 April** *P(La)* *George Selwyn, bishop, 1878*	Susanna 1–9, 15–17, 19–30, 33–62 [or 41b–62] or Joshua 2.1–14 Psalm 23 John 8.1–11	Psalms **73**, 121 or **71** Jeremiah 21.1–10 John 11.28–44	Psalms **26**, 27 or **72**, 75 Exodus 8.1–19 Hebrews 11.17–31
Tuesday	**12 April** *P(La)*	Numbers 21.4–9 Psalm 102.1–3, 16–23 John 8.21–30	Psalms **35**, 123 or **73** Jeremiah 22.1–5, 13–19 John 11.45–end	Psalms **61**, 64 or **74** Exodus 8.20–end Hebrews 11.32—12.2
Wednesday	**13 April** *P(La)*	Daniel 3.14–20, 24–25, 28 *Canticle:* Bless the Lord John 8.31–42	Psalms **55**, 124 or **77** Jeremiah 22.20—23.8 John 12.1–11	Psalms 56, **62** or **119.81**–104 Exodus 9.1–12 Hebrews 12.3–13
Thursday	**14 April** *P(La)*	Genesis 17.3–9 Psalm 105.4–9 John 8.51–end	Psalms **40**, 125 or **78.1**–39* Jeremiah 23.9–32 John 12.12–19	Psalms 42, **43** or **78.40–end** Exodus 9.13–end Hebrews 12.14–end
Friday	**15 April** *P(La)*	Jeremiah 20.10–13 Psalm 18.1–6 John 10.31–end	Psalms **22**, 126 or **55** Jeremiah 24 John 12.20–36a	Psalm **31** or **69** Exodus 10 Hebrews 13.1–16
Saturday	**16 April** *P(La)* *Isabella Gilmore, deaconess, 1923*	Ezekiel 37.21–end *Canticle:* Jeremiah 31.10–13 or Psalm 121 John 11.45–end	Psalms **23**, 127 or **76**, 79 Jeremiah 25.1–14 John 12.36b–end	Psalms 128, 129, **130** or 81, **84** Exodus 11 Hebrews 13.17–end

		Principal Service	3rd Service	2nd Service
Sunday **17 April** Palm Sunday	R	*Liturgy of the Palms:* Matthew 21.1–11 Psalm 118.1–2, 19–end [or 118.19–24] *Liturgy of the Passion:* Isaiah 50.4–9a Psalm 31.9–16 [or 9–18] Philippians 2.5–11 Matthew 26.14—end of 27 or 27.11–54	Psalms 61, 62 Zechariah 9.9–12 Luke 16.19–end	Psalm 80 Isaiah 5.1–7 Matthew 21.33–end
		Holy Communion	Morning	Evening
			From the Monday of Holy Week until the Saturday of Easter Week the seasonal psalmody must be used.	
Monday **18 April** Monday of Holy Week	R	Isaiah 42.1–9 Psalm 36.5–11 Hebrews 9.11–15 John 12.1–11	Psalm 41 Lamentations 1.1–12a Luke 22.1–23	Psalm 25 Lamentations 2.8–19 Colossians 1.18–23
Tuesday **19 April** Tuesday of Holy Week	R	Isaiah 49.1–7 Psalm 71.1–8 [9–14] 1 Corinthians 1.18–31 John 12.20–36	Psalm 27 Lamentations 3.1–18 Luke 22 [24–38] 39–53	Psalm 55.13–24 Lamentations 3.40–51 Galatians 6.11–end
Wednesday **20 April** Wednesday of Holy Week	R	Isaiah 50.4–9a Psalm 70 Hebrews 12.1–3 John 13.21–32	Psalm 102 [or 102.1–18] Wisdom 1.16—2.1, 12–22 or Jeremiah 11.18–20 Luke 22.54–end	Psalm 88 Isaiah 63.1–9 Revelation 14.18—15.4
Thursday **21 April** Maundy Thursday	W	Exodus 12.1–4 [5–10], 11–14 Psalm 116.1, 10–end [or 116.9–end] 1 Corinthians 11.23–26 John 13.1–17, 31b–35	Psalms 42, 43 Leviticus 16.2–24 Luke 23.1–25	Psalm 39 Exodus 11 Ephesians 2.11–18
Friday **22 April** Good Friday	Hangings removed; R for the Liturgy	Isaiah 52.13—end of 53 Psalm 22 or 22.1–11 [or 1–21] Hebrews 10.16–25 or 4.14–16; 5.7–9 John 18.1—end of 19	Psalm 69 Genesis 22.1–18 A part of John 18 and 19 may be read, if not used at the Principal Service or Hebrews 10.1–10	Psalms 130, 143 Lamentations 5.15–end John 19.38–end or Colossians 1.18–23

Easter

		Principal Service	3rd Service	2nd Service
Saturday	**23 April** **Easter Eve** *These readings are for use at services other than the Easter Vigil.*	*Hangings removed* Job 14.1–14 or Lamentations 3.1–9, 19–24 Psalm 31.1–4, 15–16 [1–5] 1 Peter 4.1–8 Matthew 27.57–end or John 19.38–end	Psalm 142 Hosea 6.1–6 John 2.18–22	Psalm 116 Job 19.21–27 1 John 5.5–12

		Vigil Readings	Complementary Psalmody	
Saturday **or Sunday**	**23 April evening** **24 April morning** *Easter Vigil* *The New Testament readings should be preceded by a minimum of three Old Testament readings.* *The Exodus reading should always be used.*	*Gold or W* Genesis 1.1—2.4a Genesis 7.1–5, 11–18; 8.6–18; 9.8–13 Genesis 22.1–18 **Exodus 14.10–end; 15.20–21** Isaiah 55.1–11 Baruch 3.9–15, 32—4.4 or Proverbs 8.1–8, 19–21; 9.4b–6 Ezekiel 36.24–28 Ezekiel 37.1–14 Zephaniah 3.14–end **Romans 6.3–11** **Matthew 28.1–10**	Psalm 136.1–9, 23–end Psalm 46 Psalm 16 Canticle: **Exodus 15.1b–13, 17–18** Canticle: Isaiah 12.2–end Psalm 19 Psalms 42, 43 Psalm 143 Psalm 98 **Psalm 114**	

		Principal Service	3rd Service	2nd Service
Sunday	**24 April** Easter Day	*Gold or W* Acts 10.34–43† or Jeremiah 31.1–6 Psalm 118.1–2, 14–24 [14–24] Colossians 3.1–4 or Acts 10.34–43† John 20.1–18 or Matthew 28.1–10 † *The reading from Acts must be used as either the first or second reading.*	MP Psalms 114, 117 Exodus 14.10–18, 26—15.2 Revelation 15.2–4	EP Psalms 105 or 66.1–11 Song of Solomon 3.2–5; 8.6, 7 John 20.11–18 (if not used at the Principal Service) or Revelation 1.12–18

		Holy Communion	Morning Prayer	Evening Prayer
Monday	**25 April** W Monday of Easter Week	Acts 2.14, 22–32 Psalm 16.1–2, 6–end Matthew 28.8–15	Psalms 111, 117, 146 Song of Solomon 1.9—2.7 Mark 16.1–8	Psalm 135 Exodus 12.1–14 1 Corinthians 15.1–11
Tuesday	**26 April** W Tuesday of Easter Week	Acts 2.36–41 Psalm 33.4–5, 18–end John 20.11–18	Psalms 112, 147.1–12 Song of Solomon 2.8–end Luke 24.1–12	Psalm 136 Exodus 12.14–36 1 Corinthians 15.12–19
Wednesday	**27 April** W Wednesday of Easter Week	Acts 3.1–10 Psalm 105.1–9 Luke 24.13–35	Psalms 113, 147.13–end Song of Solomon 3 Matthew 28.16–end	Psalm 105 Exodus 12.37–end 1 Corinthians 15.20–28
Thursday	**28 April** W Thursday of Easter Week	Acts 3.11–end Psalm 8 Luke 24.35–48	Psalms 114, 148 Song of Solomon 5.2—6.3 Luke 7.11–17	Psalm 106 Exodus 13.1–16 1 Corinthians 15.29–34
Friday	**29 April** W Friday of Easter Week	Acts 4.1–12 Psalm 118.1–4, 22–26 John 21.1–14	Psalms 115, 149 Song of Solomon 7.10—8.4 Luke 8.41–end	Psalm 107 Exodus 13.17—14.14 1 Corinthians 15.35–50
Saturday	**30 April** W Saturday of Easter Week	Acts 4.13–21 Psalm 118.1–4, 14–21 Mark 16.9–15	Psalms 116, 150 Song of Solomon 8.5–7 John 11.17–44	Psalm 145 Exodus 14.15–end 1 Corinthians 15.51–end

Easter 2

		Principal Service	3rd Service	2nd Service
Sunday	**1 May** **2nd Sunday of Easter** W	[Exodus 14.10–end; 15.20, 21] Acts 2.14a, 22–32† Psalm 16 1 Peter 1.3–9 John 20.19–end † *The reading from Acts must be used as either the first or second reading.*	Psalm 81.1–10 Exodus 12.1–17 1 Corinthians 5.6b–8	Psalm 30.1–5 Daniel 6.1–23 or 6.6–23 Mark 15.46–16.8 *or:* 1st EP of George, martyr, patron of England: Psalms 111, 116; Jeremiah 15.15–end; Hebrews 11.32—12.2
Monday	**2 May** R George, martyr, patron of England, c.304 *(transferred from 23 April)*	1 Maccabees 2.59–64 or Revelation 12.7–12 Psalm 126 2 Timothy 2.3–13 John 15.18–21	*MP* Psalms 5, 146 Joshua 1.1–9 Ephesians 6.10–20	*EP* Psalms 3, 11 Isaiah 43.1–7 John 15.1–8 *or:* 1st EP of Mark the Evangelist: Psalm 19; Isaiah 52.7–10; Mark 1.1–15
Tuesday	**3 May** R Mark the Evangelist *(transferred from 25 April)*	Proverbs 15.28–end or Acts 15.35–end Psalm 119.9–16 Ephesians 4.7–16 Mark 13.5–13	*MP* Psalms 37.23–end, 148 Isaiah 62.6–10 or Ecclesiasticus 51.13–end Acts 12.25—13.13	*EP* Psalm 45 Ezekiel 1.4–14 2 Timothy 4.1–11 *or:* 1st EP of Philip and James, Apostles: Psalm 25; Isaiah 40.27–end; John 12.20–26
Wednesday	**4 May** R Philip and James, Apostles *(transferred from 1 May)*	Isaiah 30.15–21 Psalm 119.1–8 Ephesians 1.3–10 John 14.1–14	*MP* Psalms 139, 146 Proverbs 4.10–18 James 1.1–12	*EP* Psalm 149 Job 23.1–12 John 1.43–end

		Holy Communion	Morning Prayer	Evening Prayer
Thursday	**5 May** W	Acts 5.27–33 Psalm 34.1, 15–end John 3.31–end	Psalms **28**, 29 or 14, **15**, 16 Deuteronomy 4.1–14 John 21.1–14	Psalm **34** or **18*** Exodus 17 Colossians 2.16—3.11
Friday	**6 May** W	Acts 5.34–42 Psalm 27.1–5, 16–17 John 6.1–15	Psalms 57, **61** or 17, **19** Deuteronomy 4.15–31 John 21.15–19	Psalm **118** or **22** Exodus 18.1–12 Colossians 3.12—4.1
Saturday	**7 May** W	Acts 6.1–7 Psalm 33.1–5, 18–19 John 6.16–21	Psalms 63, **84** or 20, 21, **23** Deuteronomy 4.32–40 John 21.20–end	Psalms **66** or **24**, 25 Exodus 18.13–end Colossians 4.2–end

		Principal Service	3rd Service	2nd Service
Sunday 8 May 3rd Sunday of Easter	W	[Zephaniah 3.14—end] Acts 2.14a, 36—41† Psalm 116.1—3, 10—end [or 1—7] 1 Peter 1.17—23 Luke 24.13—35 † The reading from Acts must be used as either the first or second reading.	Psalm 23 Isaiah 40.1—11 1 Peter 5.1—11	Psalm 48 Haggai 1.13—2.9 1 Corinthians 3.10—17 HC John 2.13—22

		Holy Communion	Morning Prayer	Evening Prayer
Monday 9 May	W	Acts 6.8—15 Psalm 119.17—24 John 6.22—29	Psalms **96**, 97 or 27, **30** Deuteronomy 5.1—22 Ephesians 1.1—14	Psalms **61**, 65 or 26, **28**, 29 Exodus 19 Luke 1.1—25
Tuesday 10 May	W	Acts 7.51—8.1a Psalm 31.1—5, 16 John 6.30—35	Psalms 98, 99, 100 or 32, **36** Deuteronomy 5.22—end Ephesians 1.15—end	Psalm 71 or 33 Exodus 20.1—21 Luke 1.26—38
Wednesday 11 May	W	Acts 8.1b—8 Psalm 66.1—6 John 6.35—40	Psalm 105 or 34 Deuteronomy 6 Ephesians 2.1—10	Psalms 67, **72** or **119.33—56** Exodus 24 Luke 1.39—56
Thursday 12 May	W	Acts 8.26—end Psalm 66.7—8, 14—end John 6.44—51	Psalm **136** or 37* Deuteronomy 7.1—11 Ephesians 2.11—end	Psalms 73 or 39, **40** Exodus 25.1—22 Luke 1.57—end
Friday 13 May	W	Acts 9.1—20 Psalm 117 John 6.52—59	Psalm 107 or 31 Deuteronomy 7.12—end Ephesians 3.1—13	Psalms 77 or 35 Exodus 28.1—4a, 29—38 Luke 2.1—20 or: 1st EP of Matthias the Apostle: Psalm 147; Isaiah 22.15—22; Philippians 3.13b—4.1

		Principal Service	3rd Service	2nd Service
Saturday 14 May Matthias the Apostle	R	Isaiah 22.15—end or Acts 1.15—end Psalm 15 Acts 1.15—end or 1 Corinthians 4.1—7 John 15.9—17	MP Psalms 16, 147.1—12 1 Samuel 2.27—35 Acts 2.37—end	EP Psalm 80 1 Samuel 16.1—13a Matthew 7.15—27

		Principal Service	3rd Service	2nd Service
Sunday	**15 May** **4th Sunday of Easter**	W	[Genesis 7] Acts 2.42–end† Psalm 23 1 Peter 2.19–end John 10.1–10 † *The reading from Acts must be used as either the first or second reading.*	Psalm 106.6–24 Nehemiah 9.6–15 1 Corinthians 10.1–13	Psalm 29.1–10 Ezra 3.1–13 Ephesians 2.11–end HC Luke 19.37–end

		Holy Communion	Morning Prayer	Evening Prayer
Monday	**16 May** *Caroline Chisholm, social reformer, 1877*	W	Acts 11.1–18 Psalms 42.1–2, 43.1–4 John 10.1–10 [or 11–18]	Psalm 103 or 44 Deuteronomy 9.1–21 Ephesians 4.1–16	Psalms 112, 113, 114 or 47, 49 Exodus 32.1–14 Luke 2.41–end
Tuesday	**17 May**	W	Acts 11.19–26 Psalm 87 John 10.22–30	Psalms 139 or 48, 52 Deuteronomy 9.23—10.5 Ephesians 4.17–end	Psalms 115, 116 or 50 Exodus 32.15–34 Luke 3.1–14
Wednesday	**18 May**	W	Acts 12.24—13.5 Psalm 67 John 12.44–end	Psalm 135 or 119.57–80 Deuteronomy 10.12–end Ephesians 5.1–14	Psalms 47, 48 or 59, 60 (67) Exodus 33 Luke 3.15–22
Thursday	**19 May** *Dunstan, archbishop, monastic reformer, 988 (see p.74)*	W	Acts 13.13–25 Psalm 89.1–2, 20–26 John 13.16–20	Psalms 118 or 56, 57 (63*) Deuteronomy 11.8–end Ephesians 5.15–end	Psalms 81, 85 or 61, 62, 64 Exodus 34.1–10, 27–end Luke 4.1–13
Friday	**20 May** *Alcuin, deacon, abbot, 804 (see p.75)*	W	Acts 13.26–33 Psalm 2 John 14.1–6	Psalms 33 or 51, 54 Deuteronomy 12.1–14 Ephesians 6.1–9	Psalms 36, 40 or 38 Exodus 35.20—36.7 Luke 4.14–30
Saturday	**21 May** *Helena, protector of the Holy Places, 330*	W	Acts 13.44–end Psalm 98.1–5 John 14.7–14	Psalm 34 or 68 Deuteronomy 15.1–18 Ephesians 6.10–end	Psalms 84, 86 or 65, 66 Exodus 40.17–end Luke 4.31–37

		Principal Service	3rd Service	2nd Service
Sunday	**22 May** **5th Sunday of Easter** W	[Genesis 8.1–19] Acts 7.55–end† Psalm 31.1–5, 15–16 [or 1–5] 1 Peter 2.2–10 John 14.1–14 † *The reading from Acts must be used* *as either the first or second reading.*	Psalm 30 Ezekiel 37.1–12 John 5.19–29	Psalm 147.1–12 Zechariah 4.1–10 Revelation 21.1–14 HC Luke 2.25–32 [33–38]

		Holy Communion	Morning Prayer	Evening Prayer
Monday	**23 May** W	Acts 14.5–18 Psalm 118.1–3, 14–15 John 14.21–26	Psalm 145 or 71 Deuteronomy 16.1–20 1 Peter 1.1–12	Psalms 105 or 72, 75 Numbers 9.15–end, 10.33–end Luke 4.38–end
Tuesday	**24 May** John and Charles Wesley, evangelists, hymn writers, 1791 and 1788 (see p. 74) W	Acts 14.19–end Psalm 145.10–end John 14.27–end	Psalms 19, 147.1–12 or 73 Deuteronomy 17.8–end 1 Peter 1.13–end	Psalms 96, 97 or 74 Numbers 11.1–33 Luke 5.1–11
Wednesday	**25 May** The Venerable Bede, monk, scholar, historian, 735 (see p. 75) Aldhelm, bishop, 709 W	Acts 15.1–6 Psalm 122.1–5 John 15.1–8	Psalms 30, 147.13–end or 77 Deuteronomy 18.9–end 1 Peter 2.1–10	Psalms 98, 99, 100 or 119.81–104 Numbers 12 Luke 5.12–26
Thursday	**26 May** Augustine, archbishop, 605 (see p. 74) John Calvin, reformer, 1564 Philip Neri, founder of the Oratorians, spiritual guide, 1595 W	Acts 15.7–21 Psalm 96.1–3, 7–10 John 15.9–11	Psalms 57, 148 or 78.1–39* Deuteronomy 19 1 Peter 2.11–end	Psalm 104 or 78.40–end* Numbers 13.1–3, 17–end Luke 5.27–end
Friday	**27 May** W	Acts 15.22–31 Psalm 57.8–end John 15.12–17	Psalms 138, 149 or 55 Deuteronomy 21.22—22.8 1 Peter 3.1–12	Psalms 66 or 69 Numbers 14.1–25 Luke 6.1–11
Saturday	**28 May** Lanfranc, monk, archbishop, scholar, 1089 W	Acts 16.1–10 Psalm 100 John 15.18–21	Psalms 146, 150 or 76, 79 Deuteronomy 24.5–end 1 Peter 3.13–end	Psalms 118 or 81, 84 Numbers 14.26–end Luke 6.12–26

	Principal Service	3rd Service	2nd Service
Sunday 29 May W **6th Sunday of Easter**	[Genesis 8.20—9.17] Acts 17.22–31† Psalm 66.7–18 1 Peter 3.13–end John 14.15–21 † *The reading from Acts must be used as either the first or second reading.*	Psalm 73.21–28 Job 14.1–2, 7–15; 19.23–27a 1 Thessalonians 4.13–end	Psalms 87, 36.5–10 Zechariah 8.1–13 Revelation 21.22—22.5 HC John 2.1–14

	Holy Communion	Morning Prayer	Evening Prayer
Monday 30 May W Josephine Butler, social reformer, 1906 (see p.76) Joan of Arc, visionary, 1431 Apolo Kivebulaya, priest, evangelist, 1933 *Rogation Day*	Acts 16.11–15 Psalm 149.1–5 John 15.26–16.4	Psalms **65**, 67 or **80**, 82 Deuteronomy 26 1 Peter 4.1–11	Psalms **121**, 122, 123 or **85**, 86 Numbers 16.1–35 Luke 6.27–38 1st EP of the Visit of the BVM to Elizabeth: Psalm 45; Song of Solomon 2.8–14; Luke 1.26–38

	Principal Service	3rd Service	2nd Service
Tuesday 31 May W Visit of the Blessed Virgin Mary to Elizabeth *Rogation Day*	Zephaniah 3.14–18 Psalm 113 Romans 12.9–16 Luke 1.39–49 [50–56]	MP Psalms **85**, 150 1 Samuel 2.1–10 Mark 3.31–end	EP Psalms 122, 127, 128 Zechariah 2.10–end John 3.25–30

	Holy Communion	Morning Prayer	Evening Prayer
Wednesday 1 June Wr Justin, martyr, c.165 (see p. 72) *Rogation Day*	Acts 17.15, 22—18.1 Psalm 148.1–2, 11–end John 16.12–15	Psalms **132**, 133 or **119**.105–128 Deuteronomy 28.58–end 1 Peter 5	**1st EP of Ascension Day:** Psalms 15, 24 2 Samuel 23.1–5 Colossians 2.20—3.4

	Principal Service	3rd Service	2nd Service
Thursday 2 June Gold or W Ascension Day	Acts 1.1–11† or Daniel 7.9–14 Psalm 47 or 93 Ephesians 1.15–end or Acts 1.1–11† Luke 24.44–end † *The reading from Acts must be used as either the first or second reading.*	MP Psalms 110, 150 Isaiah 52.7–end Hebrews 7.[11–25] 26–end	EP Psalm 8 Song of the Three vv 29–37 or 2 Kings 2.1–15 Revelation 5 HC Mark 16.14–end

		Holy Communion	Morning Prayer	Evening Prayer

The nine days after Ascension Day until the eve of Pentecost are observed as days of prayer and preparation for the celebration of the outpouring of the Holy Spirit.

From 3 – 10 June (but not 11 June, the Festival of Barnabas the Apostle), in preparation for the Day of Pentecost, an alternative sequence of daily readings for use at the one of the offices is marked with an asterisk *.

		Holy Communion	Morning Prayer	Evening Prayer
Friday 3 June *Martyrs of Uganda, 1885–7, 1977*	W	Acts 18.9–18 Psalm 47.1–6 John 16.20–23	Psalms 20, **81** or **88** (95) Deuteronomy 29.2–15 I John 1.1—2.6 *Exodus 35.30—36.1; Galatians 5.13–end	Psalm **145** or **102** Numbers 20.1–13 Luke 7.11–17
Saturday 4 June *Petroc, abbot, 6th cent.*	W	Acts 18.22–end Psalm 47.1–2, 7–end John 16.23–28	Psalms 21, **47** or 96, **97**, 100 Deuteronomy 30 I John 2.7–17 *Numbers 11.16–17, 24–29; I Corinthians 2	Psalms 84, **85** or **104** Numbers 21.4–9 Luke 7.18–35

Easter 7

	Principal Service	3rd Service	2nd Service
Sunday 5 June W **7th Sunday of Easter** *Sunday after Ascension Day*	[Ezekiel 36.24–28] Acts 1.6–14† Psalm 68.1–10 [32–35] 1 Peter 4.12–14; 5.6–11 John 17.1–11 † The reading from Acts must be used as either the first or second reading.	Psalm 104.26–35 Isaiah 65.17–end Revelation 21.1–8	Psalm 47 2 Samuel 23.1–5 Ephesians 1.15–end HC Mark 16.14–end

	Holy Communion	Morning Prayer	Evening Prayer
Monday 6 June W *Ini Kopuria, founder of the Melanesian Brotherhood, 1945*	Acts 19.1–8 Psalm 68.1–6 John 16.29–end	Psalms 93, 96, 97 or **98**, 99, 101 Deuteronomy 31.1–13 1 John 2.18–end *Numbers 27.15–end; 1 Corinthians 3*	Psalm 18 or **105*** (or 103) Numbers 22.1–35 Luke 7.36–end
Tuesday 7 June W	Acts 20.17–27 Psalm 68.9–10, 18–19 John 17.1–11	Psalms 98, **99**, 100 or **106*** (or 103) Deuteronomy 31.14–29 1 John 3.1–10 *1 Samuel 10.1–10; 1 Corinthians 12.1–13*	Psalm 68 or **107*** Numbers 22.36—23.12 Luke 8.1–15
Wednesday 8 June W *Thomas Ken, bishop, nonjuror, hymn writer, 1711 (see p. 74)*	Acts 20.28–end Psalm 68.27–28, 32–end John 17.11–19	Psalms 2, **29** or 110, 111, 112 Deuteronomy 31.30—32.14 1 John 3.11–end *1 Kings 19.1–18; Matthew 3.13–end*	Psalms 36, **46** or **119.129–152** Numbers 23.13–end Luke 8.16–25
Thursday 9 June W *Columba, abbot, missionary, 597 (see p. 75)* *Ephrem, deacon, hymn writer, teacher of the faith, 373*	Acts 22.30, 23.6–11 Psalm 16.1, 5–end John 17.20–end	Psalms 24, 72 or 113, **115** Deuteronomy 32.15–47 1 John 4.1–6 *Ezekiel 11.14–20; Matthew 9.35—10.20*	Psalms 139 or 114, **116**, 117 Numbers 24 Luke 8.26–39
Friday 10 June W	Acts 25.13–21 Psalm 103.1–2, 11–12, 19–20 John 21.15–19	Psalms 28, 30 or **139** Deuteronomy 33 1 John 4.7–end *Ezekiel 36.22–28; Matthew 12.22–32*	Psalms 147 or **130**, 131, 137 Numbers 27.12–end Luke 8.40–end or: 1st EP of Barnabas the Apostle: Psalms 1, 15; Isaiah 42.5–12; Acts 14.8–end

	Principal Service	Morning Prayer	Evening Prayer
Saturday 11 June R *Barnabas the Apostle*	Job 29.11–16 or Acts 11.19–end Psalm 112 Acts 11.19–end or Galatians 2.1–10 John 15.12–17	MP Psalms 100, 101, 117 Jeremiah 9.23–24 Acts 4.32–end	**1st EP of Pentecost:** Psalm 48 Deuteronomy 16.9–15 John 15.26—16.15

			Principal Service	3rd Service	2nd Service
Sunday	**12 June** Pentecost Whit Sunday	R	Acts 2.1–21† or Numbers 11.24–30 Psalm 104.26–36, 37b [or 26–end] 1 Corinthians 12.3b–13 or Acts 2.1–21† John 20.19–23 or John 7.37–39 † The reading from Acts must be used as either the first or second reading.	MP Psalm 87 Genesis 11.1–9 Acts 10.34–end	EP Psalms 67, 133 Joel 2.21–end Acts 2.14–21 [22–38] HC Luke 24.44–end
			Holy Communion	Morning Prayer	Evening Prayer
Monday	**13 June** Ordinary time resumes today DEL week 11	G	2 Corinthians 6.1–10 Psalm 98 Matthew 5.38–42	Psalms 123, 124, 125, **126** 2 Chronicles 17.1–12 Romans 1.1–17	Psalms **127**, 128, 129 Joshua 1 Luke 9.18–27
Tuesday	**14 June** Richard Baxter, puritan divine, 1691	G	2 Corinthians 8.1–9 Psalm 146 Matthew 5.43–end	Psalms **132**, 133 2 Chronicles 18.1–27 Romans 1.18–end	Psalms (134,) **135** Joshua 2 Luke 9.28–36
Wednesday	**15 June** Evelyn Underhill, spiritual writer, 1941	G	2 Corinthians 9.6–11 Psalm 112 Matthew 6.1–6, 16–18	Psalm 119.**153–end** 2 Chronicles 18.28—end of 19 Romans 2.1–16	Psalm **136** Joshua 3 Luke 9.37–50
Thursday	**16 June** Richard, bishop, 1253 (see p. 74) Joseph Butler, bishop, philosopher, 1752	Gw	2 Corinthians 11.1–11 Psalm 111 Matthew 6.7–15	Psalms **143**, 146 2 Chronicles 20.1–23 Romans 2.17–end	Psalms **138**, 140, 141 Joshua 4.1—5.1 Luke 9.51–end
Friday	**17 June** Samuel and Henrietta Barnett, social reformers, 1913 and 1936	G	2 Corinthians 11.18, 21b–30 Psalm 34.1–6 Matthew 6.19–23	Psalms 142, 144 2 Chronicles 22.10—end of 23 Romans 3.1–20	Psalm 145 Joshua 5.2–end Luke 10.1–16
Saturday	**18 June** Bernard Mizeki, martyr, 1896	G	2 Corinthians 12.1–10 Psalm 89.20–33 Matthew 6.24–end	Psalm **147** 2 Chronicles 24.1–22 Romans 3.21–end	1st EP of Trinity Sunday: Psalms 97, 98 Exodus 34.1–10 Mark 1.1–13

		Principal Service	3rd Service	2nd Service
Sunday	19 June Trinity Sunday	Isaiah 40.12–17, 27–end Psalm 8 2 Corinthians 13.11–end Matthew 28.16–20	MP Psalm 86.8–13 Exodus 3.1–6, 13–15 John 17.1–11	EP Psalms 93, 150 Isaiah 6.1–8 John 16.5–15
	Gold or W			
Monday	20 June DEL week 12 G	**Holy Communion** Genesis 12.1–9 Psalm 33.12–end Matthew 7.1–5	**Morning Prayer** Psalms **1**, 2, 3 2 Chronicles 26.1–21 Romans 4.1–12	**Evening Prayer** Psalms **4**, 7 Joshua 7.1–15 Luke 10.25–37
Tuesday	21 June G	Genesis 13.2, 5–end Psalm 15 Matthew 7.6, 12–14	Psalms **5**, 6 (8) 2 Chronicles 28 Romans 4.13–end	Psalms **9**, 10* Joshua 7.16–end Luke 10.38–end
Wednesday	22 June Alban, first martyr of Britain, c.250 (see p.72) Ember Day Gr	Genesis 15.1–12, 17–18 Psalm 105.1–9 Matthew 7.15–20	Psalm **119.1–32** 2 Chronicles 29.1–19 Romans 5.1–11	Psalms **11**, 12, 13 Joshua 8.1–29 Luke 11.1–13 or: 1st EP of Corpus Christi: Psalms 110, 111; Exodus 16.2–15; John 6.22–35
Thursday	23 June Day of Thanksgiving for the Institution of the Holy Communion (Corpus Christi)* W	Genesis 14.18–20 Psalm 116.10–end 1 Corinthians 11.23–26 John 6.51–58	MP Psalm 147 Deuteronomy 8.2–16 1 Corinthians 10.1–17	EP Psalms 23, 42, 43 Proverbs 9.1–5 Luke 9.11–17

Alternatively, Corpus Christi may be kept as a Lesser Festival, and either these readings or those given below may be used; or, the Lesser Festival of Etheldreda, abbess, may be kept.

		Principal Service	3rd Service	2nd Service
Thursday	23 June Day of Thanksgiving for the Institution of the Holy Communion (Corpus Christi) Etheldreda, abbess, c.678 (see p.75) Gw	Genesis 16.1–12, 15–16 Psalm 106.1–5 Matthew 7.21–end	Psalms **14**, **15**, 16 2 Chronicles 29.20–end Romans 5.12–end	Psalm **18*** Joshua 8.30–end Luke 11.14–28 or: 1st EP of the Birth of John the Baptist: Psalm 71; Judges 13.2–7, 24–end; Luke 1.5–25
Friday	24 June Birth of John the Baptist Ember Day W	Isaiah 40.1–11 Psalm 85.7–end Acts 13.14b–26 or Galatians 3.23–end Luke 1.57–66, 80	MP Psalms 50, 149 Ecclesiasticus 48.1–10 Or Malachi 3.1–6 Luke 3.1–17	EP Psalms 80, 82 Malachi 4 Matthew 11.2–19
Saturday	25 June Ember Day G	**Holy Communion** Genesis 18.1–15 Canticle: Luke 1.46b–55 Matthew 8.5–17	**Morning Prayer** Psalms **20**, 21, **23** 2 Chronicles 32.1–22 Romans 6.15–end	**Evening Prayer** Psalms **24**, 25 Joshua 10.1–15 Luke 11.37–end

		Principal Service	3rd Service	2nd Service
Sunday 26 June 1st Sunday after Trinity Proper 8	G	*Continuous:* Genesis 22.1–14 Psalm 13 *Related:* Jeremiah 28.5–9 Psalm 89.1–4, 15–18 [or 8–18] Romans 6.12–end Matthew 10.40–end	Psalms 52, 53 Deuteronomy 15.1–11 Acts 27.[13–32] 33–end	Psalm 50 [or 50.1–15] 1 Samuel 28.3–19 Luke 17.20–end

		Holy Communion	Morning Prayer	Evening Prayer
Monday 27 June *Cyril, bishop, teacher of the faith, 444* DEL week 13	G	Genesis 18.16–end Psalm 103.6–17 Matthew 8.18–22	Psalms 27, **30** 2 Chronicles 33.1–13 Romans 7.1–6	Psalms 26, **28**, 29 Joshua 14 Luke 12.1–12
Tuesday 28 June *Irenaeus, bishop, teacher of the faith, c.200* (see p. 73)	Gw	Genesis 19.15–29 Psalm 26 Matthew 8.23–27	Psalms 32, **36** 2 Chronicles 34.1–18 Romans 7.7–end	Psalm **33** Joshua 21.43—22.8 Luke 12.13–21 *or:* 1st EP of Peter and Paul, Apostles [or Peter the Apostle alone†]: Psalms 66, 67; Ezekiel 3.4–11; Galatians 1.13—2.8 [†Acts 9.32–end]

		Principal Service	3rd Service	2nd Service
Wednesday 29 June *Peter and Paul, Apostles* **or** *Peter the Apostle*	R	*Peter and Paul:* Zechariah 4.1–6a, 10b–end or Acts 12.1–11 Psalm 125 Acts 12.1–11 or 2 Timothy 4.6–8, 17–18 Matthew 16.13–19 *Peter alone:* Ezekiel 3.22–end or Acts 12.1–11 Acts 12.1–11 or 1 Peter 2.19–end Matthew 16.13–19	MP Psalms 71, 113 Isaiah 49.1–6 Acts 11.1–18	EP Psalms 124, 138 Ezekiel 34.11–16 John 21.15–22

Trinity 1

		Holy Communion	Morning Prayer	Evening Prayer
Thursday 30 June	G	Genesis 22.1–19 Psalm 116.1–7 Matthew 9.1–8	Psalm **37*** 2 Chronicles 35.1–19 Romans 8.12–17	Psalms 39, **40** Joshua 23 Luke 12.32–40
Friday 1 July *Henry, John, and Henry Venn, priests,* *evangelical divines, 1797, 1813, 1873*	G	Genesis 23.1–4, 19, 24.1–8, 62–end Psalm 106.1–5 Matthew 9.9–13	Psalm 31 2 Chronicles 35.20—36.10 Romans 8.18–30	Psalm **35** Joshua 24.1–28 Luke 12.41–48
Saturday 2 July	G	Genesis 27.1–5*a*, 15–29 Psalm 135.1–6 Matthew 9.14–17	Psalms 41, **42**, **43** 2 Chronicles 36.11–end Romans 8.31–end	Psalms 45, **46** Joshua 24.29–end Luke 12.49–end *or:* 1st EP of Thomas the Apostle: Psalm 27; Isaiah 35; Hebrews 10.35—11.1

If Thomas the Apostle is celebrated on Sunday 3 July:

		Principal Service	3rd Service	2nd Service
Sunday	R	Habakkuk 2.1–4	MP Psalms 92, 146	EP Psalm 139
3 July		Psalm 31.1–6	2 Samuel 15.17–21	Job 42.1–6
Thomas the Apostle		Ephesians 2.19–end	or Ecclesiasticus 2	1 Peter 1.3–12
		John 20.24–29	John 11.1–16	
		Holy Communion	**Morning Prayer**	**Evening Prayer**
Monday	G	Genesis 28.10–end	Psalm **44**	Psalms **47**, 49
4 July		Psalm 91.1–10	Ezra 1	Judges 2
DEL week 14		Matthew 9.18–26	Romans 9.1–18	Luke 13.1–9

If Thomas the Apostle is transferred to Monday 4 July:

		Principal Service	3rd Service	2nd Service
Sunday	G	*Continuous:*	Psalm 55.1–15, 18–22	Psalms 56 [57]
3 July		Genesis 24.34–38,	Deuteronomy 24.10–end	2 Samuel 2.1–11; 3.1
2nd Sunday after Trinity		42–49, 58–end	Acts 18.1–16	Luke 18.31 — 19.10
Proper 9		Psalm 45.10–17		or: 1st EP of Thomas the Apostle:
		or *Canticle:* Song of Solomon 2.8–13		Psalm 27; Isaiah 35;
		Romans 7.15–25a		Hebrews 10.35 — 11.1
		Matthew 11.16–19, 25–end		
		Related:		
		Zechariah 9.9–12		
		Psalm 145.8–15		
Monday	R	Habakkuk 2.1–4	MP Psalms 92, 146	EP Psalm 139
4 July		Psalm 31.1–6	2 Samuel 15.17–21	Job 42.1–6
Thomas the Apostle		Ephesians 2.19–end	or Ecclesiasticus 2	1 Peter 1.3–12
(if transferred from 3 July)		John 20.24–29	John 11.1–16	

		Holy Communion	Morning Prayer	Evening Prayer
Tuesday 5 July DEL week 14	G	Genesis 32.22–end Psalm 17.1–8 Matthew 9.32–end	Psalms **48**, 52 Ezra 3 Romans 9.19–end	Psalm **50** Judges 4.1–23 Luke 13.10–21
Wednesday 6 July *Thomas More, scholar, and John Fisher, bishop, martyrs, 1535*	G	Genesis 41.55–end, 42.5–7, 17–end Psalm 33.1–4, 18–end Matthew 10.1–7	Psalm 119.**57–80** Ezra 4.1–5 Romans 10.1–10	Psalms **59**, 60 (67) Judges 5 Luke 13.22–end
Thursday 7 July	G	Genesis 44.18–21, 23–29, 45.1–5 Psalm 105.1–17 Matthew 10.7–15	Psalms 56, **57** (63*) Ezra 4.7–end Romans 10.11–end	Psalms 61, **62**, 64 Judges 6.1–24 Luke 14.1–11
Friday 8 July	G	Genesis 46.1–7, 28–30 Psalm 37.3–6, 27–28 Matthew 10.16–23	Psalms **51**, 54 Ezra 5 Romans 11.1–12	Psalm **38** Judges 6.25–end Luke 14.12–24
Saturday 9 July	G	Genesis 49.29–end, 50.15–25 Psalm 105.1–7 Matthew 10.24–33	Psalm **68** Ezra 6 Romans 11.13–24	Psalms 65, **66** Judges 7 Luke 14.25–end

		Principal Service	3rd Service	2nd Service
Sunday	**10 July** **3rd Sunday after Trinity** Proper 10	G	*Continuous:* Genesis 25.19–end Psalm 119.105–112 Romans 8.1–end Matthew 13.1–9, 18–23 *Related:* Isaiah 55.10–13 Psalm 65.[1–7] 8–end	Psalms 64, 65 Deuteronomy 28.1–14 Acts 28.17–end	Psalms 60 [63] 2 Samuel 7.18–end Luke 19.41—20.8
			Holy Communion	**Morning Prayer**	**Evening Prayer**
Monday	**11 July** Benedict, abbot, c.550 (see p. 75) DEL week 15	Gw	Exodus 1.8–14, 22 Psalm 124 Matthew 10.34—11.1	Psalm 71 Ezra 7 Romans 11.25–end	Psalms 72, 75 Judges 8.22–end Luke 15.1–10
Tuesday	**12 July**	G	Exodus 2.1–15 Psalm 69.1–2, 31–end Matthew 11.20–24	Psalm 73 Ezra 8.15–end Romans 12.1–8	Psalm 74 Judges 9.1–21 Luke 15.11–end
Wednesday	**13 July**	G	Exodus 3.1–6, 9–12 Psalm 103.1–7 Matthew 11.25–27	Psalm 77 Ezra 9 Romans 12.9–end	Psalm 119.81–104 Judges 9.22–end Luke 16.1–18
Thursday	**14 July** John Keble, priest, poet, 1866 (see p. 74)	Gw	Exodus 3.13–20 Psalm 105.1–2, 23 Matthew 11.28–end	Psalm 78.1–39* Ezra 10.1–17 Romans 13.1–7	Psalm 78.40–end* Judges 11.1–11 Luke 16.19–end
Friday	**15 July** Swithun, bishop, c.862 (see p. 74) *Bonaventure, friar, bishop,* *teacher of the faith, 1274*	Gw	Exodus 11.10—12.14 Psalm 116.10–end Matthew 12.1–8	Psalm 55 Nehemiah 1 Romans 13.8–end	Psalm 69 Judges 11.29–end Luke 17.1–10
Saturday	**16 July** *Osmund, bishop, 1099*	G	Exodus 12.37–42 Psalm 136.1–4, 10–15 Matthew 12.14–21	Psalms 76, 79 Nehemiah 2 Romans 14.1–12	Psalms 81, 84 Judges 12.1–7 Luke 17.11–19

49

Trinity 4

	Principal Service	3rd Service	2nd Service
Sunday 17 July G **4th Sunday after Trinity** Proper 11	*Continuous:* Genesis 28.10–19a Psalm 139.1–11, 23–24 [or 1–11] *Related:* Wisdom of Solomon 12.13, 16–19 or Isaiah 44.6–8 Psalm 86.11–17 Romans 8.12–25 Matthew 13.24–30, 36–43	Psalm 71 Deuteronomy 30.1–10 1 Peter 3.8–18	Psalms 67 [70] 1 Kings 2.10–12; 3.16–end Acts 4.1–22 HC Mark 6.30–34, 53–end

	Holy Communion	Morning Prayer	Evening Prayer
Monday 18 July G Elizabeth Ferard, deaconess, founder of the Community of St Andrew, 1883 DEL week 16	Exodus 14.5–18 Psalm 136.1–4, 10–15 or Canticle: Exodus 15.1–6 Matthew 12.38–42	Psalms 80, 82 Nehemiah 4 Romans 14.13–end	Psalms 85, 86 Judges 13.1–24 Luke 17.20–end
Tuesday 19 July Gw Gregory, bishop, and his sister Macrina, deaconess, teachers of the faith, c.394 and c.379 (see p. 73)	Exodus 14.21—15.1 Psalm 105.37–44 or Canticle: Exodus 15.8–10, 12, 17 Matthew 12.46–end	Psalms 87, **89.1–18** Nehemiah 5 Romans 15.1–13	Psalm **89.19–end** Judges 14 Luke 18.1–14
Wednesday 20 July G Margaret of Antioch, martyr, 4th cent. Bartolomé de las Casas, Apostle to the Indies, 1566	Exodus 16.1–5, 9–15 Psalm 78.17–31 Matthew 13.1–9	Psalm 1**119.105–128** Nehemiah 6.1—7.4 Romans 15.14–21	Psalms 91, 93 Judges 15.1—16.3 Luke 18.15–30
Thursday 21 July G	Exodus 19.1–2, 9–11, 16–20 Canticle: Bless the Lord Matthew 13.10–17	Psalms 90, **92** Nehemiah 7.73b–end of 8 Romans 15.22–end	Psalm **94** Judges 16.4–end Luke 18.31–end or: 1st EP of Mary Magdalene: Psalm 139; Isaiah 25.1–9; 2 Corinthians 1.3–7

	Principal Service	3rd Service	2nd Service
Friday 22 July W Mary Magdalene	Song of Solomon 3.1–4 Psalm 42.1–10 2 Corinthians 5.14–17 John 20.1–2, 11–18	MP Psalms 30, 32, 150 1 Samuel 16.14–end Luke 8.1–3	EP Psalm 63 Zephaniah 3.14–end Mark 15.40—16.7

	Holy Communion	Morning Prayer	Evening Prayer
Saturday 23 July G Bridget, abbess, 1373	Exodus 24.3–8 Psalm 50.1–6, 14–15 Matthew 13.24–30	Psalms 96, **97**, 100 Nehemiah 9.24–end Romans 16.17–end	Psalm 104 Judges 18.1–20, 27–end Luke 19.11–27

	Principal Service	3rd Service	2nd Service
Sunday 24 July **5th Sunday after Trinity** Proper 12 G	*Continuous:* Genesis 29.15–28 Psalm 105.1–11, 45b [or 1–11] or Psalm 128 *Related:* 1 Kings 3.5–12 Psalm 119.129–136 Romans 8.26–end Matthew 13.31–33, 44–52	Psalm 77 Song of Solomon 2 or 1 Maccabees 2.[1–14] 15–22 1 Peter 4.7–14	Psalms 75 [76] 1 Kings 6.11–14, 23–end Acts 12.1–17 HC John 6.1–21 or: 1st EP of James the Apostle: Psalm 144; Deuteronomy 30.11–end; Mark 5.21–end
Monday 25 July James the Apostle R	Jeremiah 45.1–5 or Acts 11.27—12.2 Psalm 126 Acts 11.27—12.2 or 2 Corinthians 4.7–15 Matthew 20.20–28	MP Psalms 7, 29, 117 2 Kings 1.9–15 Luke 9.46–56	EP Psalm 94 Jeremiah 26.1–15 Mark 1.14–20
	Holy Communion	**Morning Prayer**	**Evening Prayer**
Tuesday 26 July Anne and Joachim, parents of the Blessed Virgin Mary DEL week 17 Gw	Exodus 33.7–11, 34.5–9, 28 Psalm 103.8–12 Matthew 13.36–43 *Lesser Festival eucharistic lectionary:* Zephaniah 3.14–18a; Psalm 127; Romans 8.28–30; Matthew 13.16–17	Psalm 106* (or 103) Nehemiah 13.1–14 2 Corinthians 1.15—2.4	Psalm 107* 1 Samuel 1.21—2.11 Luke 19.41–end
Wednesday 27 July Brooke Foss Westcott, bishop, teacher of the faith, 1901 G	Exodus 34.29–end Psalm 99 Matthew 13.44–46	Psalms 110, 111, 112 Nehemiah 13.15–end 2 Corinthians 2.5–end	Psalm 119.129–152 1 Samuel 2.12–26 Luke 20.1–8
Thursday 28 July G	Exodus 40.16–21, 34–end Psalm 84.1–6 Matthew 13.47–53	Psalms 113, 115 Esther 1 2 Corinthians 3	Psalms 114, 116, 117 1 Samuel 2.27–end Luke 20.9–19
Friday 29 July Mary, Martha and Lazarus, companions of Our Lord Gw	Leviticus 23.1, 4–11, 15–16, 27, 34–37 Psalm 81.1–8 Matthew 13.54–end *Lesser Festival eucharistic lectionary:* Isaiah 25.6–9; Psalm 49.5–10, 16; Hebrews 2.10–15; John 12.1–8	Psalm 139 Esther 2 2 Corinthians 4	Psalms 130, 131, 137 1 Samuel 3.1—4.1a Luke 20.20–26
Saturday 30 July William Wilberforce, social reformer, 1833 (see p. 76) Gw	Leviticus 25.1, 8–17 Psalm 67 Matthew 14.1–12	Psalms 120, 121, 122 Esther 3 2 Corinthians 5	Psalm 118 1 Samuel 4.1b–end Luke 20.27–40

Trinity 6

	Principal Service	3rd Service	2nd Service
Sunday **31 July** **6th Sunday after Trinity** Proper 13	G		
	Continuous: Genesis 32.22–31 Psalm 17.1–7,16 [or 1–7] Related: Isaiah 55.1–5 Psalm 145.8–9, 15–end [or 15–end] Romans 9.1–5 Matthew 14.13–21	Psalm 85 Song of Solomon 5.2–end or 1 Maccabees 3.1–12 2 Peter 1.1–15	Psalm 80 [or 80.1–8] 1 Kings 10.1–13 Acts 13.1–13 HC John 6.24–35
	Holy Communion	**Morning Prayer**	**Evening Prayer**
Monday **1 August** DEL week 18	G Numbers 11.4–15 Psalm 81.1–end Matthew 14.13–21	Psalms 123, 124, 125, **126** Esther 4 2 Corinthians 6.1—7.1	Psalms **127**, 128, 129 1 Samuel 5 Luke 20.41—21.4
Tuesday **2 August**	G Numbers 12.1–13 Psalm 51.1–8 Matthew 14.22–end or 15.1–2, 10–14	Psalms **132**, 133 Esther 5 2 Corinthians 7.2–end	Psalms (134,) **135** 1 Samuel 6.1–16 Luke 21.5–19
Wednesday **3 August**	G Numbers 13.1–2, 25—14.1, 26–35 Psalm 106.14–24 Matthew 15.21–28	Psalm **119.153–end** Esther 6.1–13 2 Corinthians 8.1–15	Psalm **136** 1 Samuel 7 Luke 21.20–28
Thursday **4 August** Jean-Baptiste Vianney, curé d'Ars, spiritual guide, 1859	G Numbers 20.1–13 Psalm 95.1, 8–end Matthew 16.13–23	Psalms **143**, 146 Esther 6.14—end of 7 2 Corinthians 8.16—9.5	Psalms **138**, 140, 141 1 Samuel 8 Luke 21.29–end
Friday **5 August** Oswald, king, martyr, 642 (see p.72)	Gr Deuteronomy 4.32–40 Psalm 77.11–end Matthew 16.24–end	Psalms 142, **144** Esther 8 2 Corinthians 9.6–end	Psalm **145** 1 Samuel 9.1–14 Luke 22.1–13 or: 1st EP of the Transfiguration of Our Lord: Psalms 99, 110; Exodus 24.12–end; John 12.27–36a
	Principal Service	**3rd Service**	**2nd Service**
Saturday **6 August** Transfiguration of Our Lord	Gold or W Daniel 7.9–10, 13–14 Psalm 97 2 Peter 1.16–19 Luke 9.28–36	MP Psalms 27, 150 Ecclesiasticus 48.1–10 or 1 Kings 19.1–16 1 John 3.1–3	EP Psalm 72 Exodus 34.29–end 2 Corinthians 3

		Principal Service		3rd Service	2nd Service
Sunday	**7 August** G **7th Sunday after Trinity** Proper 14	*Continuous:* Genesis 37.1–4, 12–28 Psalm 105.1–6, 16–22, 45b [or 1–10]	*Related:* 1 Kings 19.9–18 Psalm 85.8–13	Psalm 88 Song of Solomon 8.5–7 or 1 Maccabees 14.4–15 2 Peter 3.8–13	Psalm 86 1 Kings 11.41—12.20 Acts 14.8–20 HC John 6.35, 41–51
		Romans 10.5–15 Matthew 14.22–33			
		Holy Communion		**Morning Prayer**	**Evening Prayer**
Monday	**8 August** Gw Dominic, priest, founder of the Order of Preachers, 1221 (see p. 75) DEL week 19	Deuteronomy 10.12–end Psalm 147.13–end Matthew 17.22–end		Psalms 1, 2, 3 Jeremiah 26 2 Corinthians 11.1–15	Psalms **4**, 7 1 Samuel 10.1–16 Luke 22.24–30
Tuesday	**9 August** Gw Mary Sumner, founder of the Mothers' Union, 1921 (see p. 76)	Deuteronomy 31.1–8 Psalm 107.1–3, 42–end or Canticle: Deuteronomy 32.3–4, 7–9 Matthew 18.1–5, 10, 12–14		Psalms **5**, 6 (8) Jeremiah 28 2 Corinthians 11.16–end	Psalms **9**, 10* 1 Samuel 10.17–end Luke 22.31–38
Wednesday	**10 August** Gr Laurence, deacon, martyr, 258 (see p. 72)	Deuteronomy 34 Psalm 66.14–end Matthew 18.15–20		Psalm 119.1–**32** Jeremiah 29.1–14 2 Corinthians 12	Psalms **11**, 12, 13 1 Samuel 11 Luke 22.39–46
Thursday	**11 August** Gw Clare of Assisi, founder of the Poor Clares, 1253 (see p. 75) John Henry Newman, priest, 1890	Joshua 3.7–11, 13–17 Psalm 114 Matthew 18.21—19.1		Psalms 14, **15**, 16 Jeremiah 30.1–11 2 Corinthians 13	Psalm 18* 1 Samuel 12 Luke 22.47–62
Friday	**12 August** G	Joshua 24.1–13 Psalm 136.1–3, 16–22 Matthew 19.3–12		Psalms 17, **19** Jeremiah 30.12–22 James 1.1–11	Psalm **22** 1 Samuel 13.5–18 Luke 22.63–end
Saturday	**13 August** Gw Jeremy Taylor, bishop, teacher of the faith, 1667 (see p. 73) Florence Nightingale, nurse, social reformer, 1910 Octavia Hill, social reformer, 1912	Joshua 24.14–29 Psalm 16.1, 5–end Matthew 19.13–15		Psalms 20, 21, **23** Jeremiah 31.1–22 James 1.12–end	Psalms **24**, 25 1 Samuel 13.19—14.15 Luke 23.1–12

Trinity 8

Sunday 14 August — 8th Sunday after Trinity (G), Proper 15

	Principal Service	3rd Service	2nd Service
Sunday 14 August 8th Sunday after Trinity Proper 15	*Continuous:* Genesis 45.1–15 Psalm 133 *Related:* Isaiah 56.1, 6–8 Psalm 67 Romans 11.1–2a, 29–32 Matthew 15.[10–20] 21–28	Psalm 92 Jonah 1 or Ecclesiasticus 3.1–15 2 Peter 3.14–end	Psalm 90 [or 90.1–12] 2 Kings 4.1–37 Acts 16.1–15 HC John 6.51–58 or: 1st EP of the Blessed Virgin Mary: Psalm 72; Proverbs 8.22–31; John 19.23–27
Monday 15 August The Blessed Virgin Mary (W)	Isaiah 61.10–end or Revelation 11.19—12.6, 10 Psalm 45.10–end Galatians 4.4–7 Luke 1.46–55	MP Psalms 98, 138, 147.1–12 Isaiah 7.10–15 Luke 11.27–28	EP Psalm 132 Song of Solomon 2.1–7 Acts 1.6–14

	Holy Communion	Morning Prayer	Evening Prayer
Tuesday 16 August (G) DEL week 20	Judges 6.11–24 Psalm 85.8–end Matthew 19.23–end	Psalms 32, 36 Jeremiah 32.1–15 James 2.14–end	Psalm 33 1 Samuel 15.1–23 Luke 23.26–43
Wednesday 17 August (G)	Judges 9.6–15 Psalm 21.1–6 Matthew 20.1–16	Psalm 34 Jeremiah 33.1–13 James 3	Psalm 119.33–56 1 Samuel 16 Luke 23.44–56a
Thursday 18 August (G)	Judges 11.29–end Psalm 40.4–11 Matthew 22.1–14	Psalm 37* Jeremiah 33.14–end James 4.1–12	Psalms 39, 40 1 Samuel 17.1–30 Luke 23.56b–24.12
Friday 19 August (G)	Ruth 1.1, 3–6, 14–16, 22 Psalm 146 Matthew 22.34–40	Psalm 31 Jeremiah 35 James 4.13—5.6	Psalm 35 1 Samuel 17.31–54 Luke 24.13–35
Saturday 20 August (Gw) Bernard, abbot, teacher of the faith, 1153 (see p. 73); William and Catherine Booth, founders of the Salvation Army, 1912, 1890	Ruth 2.1–3, 8–11; 4.13–17 Psalm 128 Matthew 23.1–12	Psalms 41, 42, 43 Jeremiah 36.1–18 James 5.7–end	Psalms 45, 46 1 Samuel 17.55—18.16 Luke 24.36–end

		Principal Service	3rd Service	2nd Service
Sunday 21 August 9th Sunday after Trinity Proper 16	G	*Continuous:* Exodus 1.8—2.10 Psalm 124 *Related:* Isaiah 51.1–6 Psalm 138 Romans 12.1–8 Matthew 16.13–20	Psalm 104.1–25 Jonah 2 or Ecclesiasticus 3.17–29 Revelation 1	Psalm 95 2 Kings 6.8–23 Acts 17.15–end HC John 6.56–69
		Holy Communion	**Morning Prayer**	**Evening Prayer**
Monday 22 August DEL week 21	G	1 Thessalonians 1.1–5, 8–end Psalm 149.1–5 Matthew 23.13–22	Psalm 44 Jeremiah 36.19–end Mark 1.1–13	Psalms 47, 49 1 Samuel 19.1–18 Acts 1.1–14
Tuesday 23 August	G	1 Thessalonians 2.1–8 Psalm 139.1–9 Matthew 23.23–26	Psalms 48, 52 Jeremiah 37 Mark 1.14–20	Psalm 50 1 Samuel 20.1–17 Acts 1.15–end *or:* 1st EP of Bartholomew the Apostle: Psalm 97; Isaiah 61.1–9; 2 Corinthians 6.1–10
		Principal Service	**3rd Service**	**2nd Service**
Wednesday 24 August Bartholomew the Apostle	R	Isaiah 43.8–13 or Acts 5.12–16 Psalm 145.1–7 Acts 5.12–16 or 1 Corinthians 4.9–15 Luke 22.24–30	MP Psalms 86, 117 Genesis 28.10–17 John 1.43–end	EP Psalms 91, 116 Ecclesiasticus 39.1–10 or Deuteronomy 18.15–19 Matthew 10.1–22
		Holy Communion	**Morning Prayer**	**Evening Prayer**
Thursday 25 August	G	1 Thessalonians 3.7–end Psalm 90.13–end Matthew 24.42–end	Psalms 56, **57** (63*) Jeremiah 38.14–end Mark 1.29–end	Psalms 61, **62**, 64 1 Samuel 21.1—22.5 Acts 2.22–36
Friday 26 August	G	1 Thessalonians 4.1–8 Psalm 97 Matthew 25.1–13	Psalms **51**, 54 Jeremiah 39 Mark 2.1–12	Psalm 38 1 Samuel 22.6–end Acts 2.37–end
Saturday 27 August Monica, mother of Augustine of Hippo, 387 (see p. 76)	Gw	1 Thessalonians 4.9–12 Psalm 98.1–2, 8–end Matthew 25.14–30	Psalm **68** Jeremiah 40 Mark 2.13–22	Psalms 65, **66** 1 Samuel 23 Acts 3.1–10

		Principal Service		2nd Service
Sunday	28 August **10th Sunday after Trinity** Proper 17	*Continuous:* Exodus 3.1–15 Psalm 105.1–6, 23–26, 45b [or Psalm 115]	*Related:* Jeremiah 15.15–21 Psalm 26.1–8 Romans 12.9–end Matthew 16.21–end	Psalm 105.1–15 2 Kings 6.24–25; 7.3–end Acts 18.1–16 HC Mark 7.1–8, 14, 15, 21–23

		Holy Communion	Morning Prayer	Evening Prayer
Monday	29 August Gr Beheading of John the Baptist DEL week 22	1 Thessalonians 4.13–end Psalm 96 Luke 4.16–30 *Lesser Festival eucharistic lectionary:* Jeremiah 1.4–10; Psalm 11; Hebrews 11.32—12.2; Matthew 14.1–12	Psalm 71 Jeremiah 41 Mark 2.23—3.6	Psalms 72, 75 1 Samuel 24 Acts 3.11–end
Tuesday	30 August Gw John Bunyan, spiritual writer, 1688 (see p. 73)	1 Thessalonians 5.1–6, 9–11 Psalm 27.1–8 Luke 4.31–37	Psalm 73 Jeremiah 42 Mark 3.7–19a	Psalm 74 1 Samuel 26 Acts 4.1–12
Wednesday	31 August Gw Aidan, bishop, missionary, 651 (see p. 75)	Colossians 1.1–8 Psalm 34.11–18 Luke 4.38–end	Psalm 77 Jeremiah 43 Mark 3.19b–end	Psalm 119.81–104 1 Samuel 28.3–end Acts 4.13–31
Thursday	1 September G *Giles, hermit, c.710*	Colossians 1.9–14 Psalm 98.1–5 Luke 5.1–11	Psalm 78.1–39* Jeremiah 44.1–14 Mark 4.1–20	Psalm 78.40–end* 1 Samuel 31 Acts 4.32—5.11
Friday	2 September G *Martyrs of Papua New Guinea, 1901, 1942*	Colossians 1.15–20 Psalm 89.19b–28 Luke 5.33–end	Psalm 55 Jeremiah 44.15–end Mark 4.21–34	Psalm 69 2 Samuel 1 Acts 5.12–26
Saturday	3 September Gw Gregory the Great, bishop, teacher of the faith, 604 (see p. 73)	Colossians 1.21–23 Psalm 117 Luke 6.1–5	Psalms 76, 79 Jeremiah 45 Mark 4.35–end	Psalms 81, 84 2 Samuel 2.1–11 Acts 5.27–end

		3rd Service
Sunday		Psalm 107.1–32 Jonah 3.1–9 or Ecclesiasticus 11.7–28 [or 19–28] Revelation 3.14–end

		Principal Service	3rd Service	2nd Service
Sunday	**4 September** G **11th Sunday after Trinity** Proper 18	*Continuous:* Exodus 12.1–14 Psalm 149 *Related:* Ezekiel 33.7–11 Psalm 119.33–40 Romans 13.8–end Matthew 18.15–20	Psalm 119.17–32 Jonah 3.10—4.11 or Ecclesiasticus 27.30—28.9 Revelation 8.1–5	Psalms 108 [115] Ezekiel 12.21—13.16 Acts 19.1–20 HC Mark 7.24–end
		Holy Communion	**Morning Prayer**	**Evening Prayer**
Monday	**5 September** G DEL week 23	Colossians 1.24—2.3 Psalm 62.1–7 Luke 6.6–11	Psalms 80, 82 Micah 1.1–9 Mark 5.1–20	Psalms 85, 86 2 Samuel 3.12–end Acts 6
Tuesday	**6 September** G *Allen Gardiner, missionary, founder of the South American Mission Society, 1851*	Colossians 2.6–15 Psalm 8 Luke 6.12–19	Psalms 87, **89.1–18** Micah 2 Mark 5.21–34	Psalm **89.19–end** 2 Samuel 5.1–12 Acts 7.1–16
Wednesday	**7 September** G	Colossians 3.1–11 Psalm 15 Luke 6.20–26	Psalm **119.105–128** Micah 3 Mark 5.35–end	Psalms **91**, 93 2 Samuel 6.1–19 Acts 7.17–43
Thursday	**8 September** Gw Birth of the Blessed Virgin Mary (see p.72)	Colossians 3.12–17 Psalm 149.1–5 Luke 6.27–38	Psalms 90, **92** Micah 4.1—5.1 Mark 6.1–13	Psalm **94** 2 Samuel 7.1–17 Acts 7.44–53
Friday	**9 September** G *Charles Fuge Lowder, priest, 1880*	1 Timothy 1.1–2, 12–14 Psalm 16 Luke 6.39–42	Psalms 88 (95) Micah 5.2–end Mark 6.14–29	Psalm 102 2 Samuel 7.18–end Acts 7.54—8.3
Saturday	**10 September** G	1 Timothy 1.15–17 Psalm 113 Luke 6.43–end	Psalms 96, **97**, 100 Micah 6 Mark 6.30–44	Psalm 104 2 Samuel 9 Acts 8.4–25

57

Trinity 12

	Principal Service	3rd Service	2nd Service
Sunday 11 September G 12th Sunday after Trinity, Proper 19	*Continuous:* Exodus 14.19–end; Psalm 114 or *Canticle:* Exodus 15.1b–11, 20, 21; Romans 14.1–12; Matthew 18.21–35 — *Related:* Genesis 50.15–21; Psalm 103.[1–7] 8–13	Psalm 119.65–88; Isaiah 44.24—45.8; Revelation 12.1–12	Psalm 119.41–48 [49–64]; Ezekiel 20.1–8, 33–44; Acts 20.17–end; HC Mark 8.27–end

	Holy Communion	Morning Prayer	Evening Prayer
Monday 12 September G DEL week 24	1 Timothy 2.1–8; Psalm 28; Luke 7.1–10	Psalms 98, 99, 101; Micah 7.1–7; Mark 6.45–end	Psalm 105* (or 103); 2 Samuel 11; Acts 8.26–end
Tuesday 13 September Gw John Chrysostom, bishop, teacher of the faith, 407 (see p. 73)	1 Timothy 3.1–13; Psalm 101; Luke 7.11–17	Psalms 106* (or 103); Micah 7.8–end; Mark 7.1–13	Psalm 107*; 2 Samuel 12.1–25; Acts 9.1–19a **or:** 1st EP of Holy Cross Day: Psalm 66; Isaiah 52.13—end of 53; Ephesians 2.11–end

	Principal Service	3rd Service	2nd Service
Wednesday 14 September R Holy Cross Day	Numbers 21.4–9; Psalm 22.23–28; Philippians 2.6–11; John 3.13–17	MP Psalms 2, 8, 146; Genesis 3.1–15; John 12.27–36a	EP Psalms 110, 150; Isaiah 63.1–16; 1 Corinthians 1.18–25

	Holy Communion	Morning Prayer	Evening Prayer
Thursday 15 September Gr Cyprian, bishop, martyr, 258 (see p. 72)	1 Timothy 4.12–end; Psalm 111.6–end; Luke 7.36–end	Psalms 113, **115**; Habakkuk 1.12—2.5; Mark 7.24–30	Psalms 114, **116**, 117; 2 Samuel 15.13–end; Acts 9.32–end
Friday 16 September Gw Ninian, bishop, apostle of the Picts, c.432 (see p. 75); Edward Bouverie Pusey, priest, 1882	1 Timothy 6.2b–12; Psalm 49.1–9; Luke 8.1–3	Psalm 139; Habakkuk 2.6–end; Mark 7.31–end	Psalms 130, 131, 137; 2 Samuel 16.1–14; Acts 10.1–16
Saturday 17 September Gw Hildegard, abbess, visionary, 1179 (see p. 75)	1 Timothy 6.13–16; Psalm 100; Luke 8.4–15	Psalms 120, **121**, 122; Habakkuk 3.2–19a; Mark 8.1–10	Psalm 118; 2 Samuel 17.1–23; Acts 10.17–33

	Principal Service	3rd Service	2nd Service
Sunday 18 September G 13th Sunday after Trinity Proper 20	*Continuous:* Exodus 16.2–15; Psalm 105.1–6, 37–end [or 37–end] *Related:* Jonah 3.10—end of 4; Psalm 145.1–8 Philippians 1.21–end Matthew 20.1–16	Psalm 119.153–end Isaiah 45.9–22 Revelation 14.1–5	Psalm 119.113–136 [or 121–128] Ezekiel 33.23, 30—34.10 Acts 26.1, 9–25 HC Mark 9.30–37

	Holy Communion	Morning Prayer	Evening Prayer
Monday 19 September G *Theodore, archbishop, 690* DEL week 25	Ezra 1.1–6 Psalm 126 Luke 8.16–18	Psalms 123, 124, 125, **126** Haggai 1.1—11 Mark 8.11–21	Psalms **127**, 128, 129 2 Samuel 18.1–18 Acts 10.34–end
Tuesday 20 September Gr John Coleridge Patteson, bishop, and companions, martyrs, 1871 (see p. 72)	Ezra 6.7–8, 12, 14–20 Psalm 124 Luke 8.19–21	Psalms **132**, 133 Haggai 1.12—2.9 Mark 8.22–26	Psalms (134), **135** 2 Samuel 18.19—19.8a Acts 11.1–18 *or: 1st EP of Matthew, Apostle and Evangelist:* Psalm 34; Isaiah 33.13–17; Matthew 6.19–end

	Principal Service	3rd Service	2nd Service
Wednesday 21 September R Matthew, Apostle and Evangelist	Proverbs 3.13–18 Psalm 119.65–72 2 Corinthians 4.1–6 Matthew 9.9–13	*MP* Psalms 49, 117 1 Kings 19.15–end 2 Timothy 3.14–end	*EP* Psalm 119.33–40, 89–96 Ecclesiastes 5.4–12 Matthew 19.16–end

	Holy Communion	Morning Prayer	Evening Prayer
Thursday 22 September G	Haggai 1.1–8 Psalm 149.1–5 Luke 9.7–9	Psalms **143**, 146 Zechariah 1.1–17 Mark 9.2–13	Psalms **138**, 140, 141 2 Samuel 19.24–end Acts 12.1–17
Friday 23 September G	Haggai 1.15b—2.9 Psalm 43 Luke 9.18–22	Psalms 142, **144** Zechariah 1.18—end of 2 Mark 9.14–29	Psalm **145** 2 Samuel 23.1–7 Acts 12.18–end
Saturday 24 September G	Zechariah 2.1–5, 10–11 Psalm 125 or *Canticle:* Jeremiah 31.10–13 Luke 9.43b–45	Psalm **147** Zechariah 3 Mark 9.30–37	Psalms **148**, 149, 150 2 Samuel 24 Acts 13.1–12

Trinity 14

	Principal Service	3rd Service	2nd Service
Sunday 25 September G **14th Sunday after Trinity** Proper 21	*Continuous:* Exodus 17.1–7 Psalm 78.1–4, 12–16 [or 1–7] *Related:* Ezekiel 18.1–4, 25–end Psalm 25.1–8 Philippians 2.1–13 Matthew 21.23–32	Psalms 125, 126, 127 Isaiah 48.12–21 Luke 11.37–54	Psalms [120, 123] 124 Ezekiel 37.15–end 1 John 2.22–end HC Mark 9.38–end

	Holy Communion	Morning Prayer	Evening Prayer
Monday 26 September G Wilson Carlile, *founder of the Church Army, 1942* DEL week 26	Zechariah 8.1–8 Psalm 102.12–22 Luke 9.46–50	Psalms 1, 2, 3 Zechariah 4 Mark 9.38–end	Psalms 4, 7 1 Kings 1.5–31 Acts 13.13–43
Tuesday 27 September Gw Vincent de Paul, *founder of the Lazarists, 1660 (see p.75)*	Zechariah 8.20–end Psalm 87 Luke 9.51–56	Psalms 5, 6 (8) Zechariah 6.9–end Mark 10.1–16	Psalms 9, 10* 1 Kings 1.32—2.4; 2.10–12 Acts 13.44—14.7
Wednesday 28 September G Ember Day	Nehemiah 2.1–8 Psalm 137.1–6 Luke 9.57–end	Psalm 119.1–32 Zechariah 7 Mark 10.17–31	Psalms 11, 12, 13 1 Kings 3 Acts 14.8–end *or:* 1st EP of Michael and All Angels: Psalm 91; 2 Kings 6.8–17; Matthew 18.1–6, 10

	Principal Service	3rd Service	2nd Service
Thursday 29 September W **Michael and All Angels**	Genesis 28.10–17 or Revelation 12.7–12 Psalm 103.19–end Revelation 12.7–12 or Hebrews 1.5–end John 1.47–end	MP Psalms 34, 150 Tobit 12.6–end or Daniel 12.1–4 Acts 12.1–11	EP Psalms 138, 148 Daniel 10.4–end Revelation 5

	Holy Communion	Morning Prayer	Evening Prayer
Friday 30 September G Jerome, *translator, teacher of the faith, 420* Ember Day	Baruch 1.15–end or Deuteronomy 31.7–13 Psalm 79.1–9 Luke 10.13–16	Psalms 17, 19 Zechariah 8.9–end Mark 10.35–45	Psalm 22 1 Kings 6.1, 11–28 Acts 15.22–35
Saturday 1 October G Remigius, *bishop, 533* Anthony Ashley Cooper (Earl of Shaftesbury), *social reformer, 1885* Ember Day	Baruch 4.5–12, 27–29 or Joshua 22.1–6 Psalm 69.33–37 Luke 10.17–24	Psalms 20, 21, 23 Zechariah 9.1–12 Mark 10.46–end	Psalms 24, 25 1 Kings 8.1–30 Acts 15.36—16.5

		Principal Service	3rd Service	2nd Service
Sunday	**2 October** G 15th Sunday after Trinity Proper 22	*Continuous:* Exodus 20.1–4, 7–9, 12–20 Psalm 19 [or 19.7–end] *Related:* Isaiah 5.1–7 Psalm 80.9–17 Philippians 3.4b–14 Matthew 21.33–end	Psalms 128, 129, 134 Isaiah 49.13–23 Luke 12.1–12	Psalm 136 [or 136.1–9] Proverbs 2.1–11 1 John 2.1–17 HC Mark 10.2–16
		Holy Communion	**Morning Prayer**	**Evening Prayer**
Monday	**3 October** G DEL week 27	Jonah 1.1 — 2.2, 10 *Canticle:* Jonah 2.2–4, 7 or Psalm 69.1–6 Luke 10.25–37	Psalms 27, **30** Zechariah 10 Mark 11.1–11	Psalms 26, **28**, 29 1 Kings 8.31–62 Acts 16.6–24
Tuesday	**4 October** Gw Francis of Assisi, friar, deacon, 1226 (see p. 75)	Jonah 3 Psalm 130 Luke 10.38–end	Psalms 32, **36** Zechariah 11.4–end Mark 11.12–26	Psalm 33 1 Kings 8.63 — 9.9 Acts 16.25–end
Wednesday	**5 October** G	Jonah 4 Psalm 86.1–9 Luke 11.1–4	Psalm **34** Zechariah 12.1–10 Mark 11.27–end	Psalm 1**19.33–56** 1 Kings 10.1–25 Acts 17.1–15
Thursday	**6 October** Gr William Tyndale, translator, martyr, 1536 (see p. 72)	Malachi 3.13 — 4.2*a* Psalm 1 Luke 11.5–13	Psalm **37*** Zechariah 13 Mark 12.1–12	Psalms 39, **40** 1 Kings 11.1–13 Acts 17.16–end
Friday	**7 October** G	Joel 1.13–15, 2.1–2 Psalm 9.1–7 Luke 11.15–26	Psalm 31 Zechariah 14.1–11 Mark 12.13–17	Psalm 35 1 Kings 11.26–end Acts 18.1–21
Saturday	**8 October** G	Joel 3.12–end Psalm 97.1, 8–end Luke 11.27–28	Psalms 41, **42**, 43 Zechariah 14.12–end Mark 12.18–27	Psalms 45, **46** 1 Kings 12.1–24 Acts 18.22 —19.7

Trinity 16

		Principal Service		3rd Service	2nd Service
Sunday 9 October **16th Sunday after Trinity** Proper 23	G	*Continuous:* Exodus 32.1–14 Psalm 106.1–6, 19–23 [or 1–6] Philippians 4.1–9 Matthew 22.1–14	*Related:* Isaiah 25.1–9 Psalm 23	Psalms 138, 141 Isaiah 50.4–10 Luke 13.22–30	Psalm 139.1–18 [or 1–11] Proverbs 3.1–18 1 John 3.1–15 HC Mark 10.17–31
		Holy Communion		**Morning Prayer**	**Evening Prayer**
Monday 10 October *Paulinus*, bishop, missionary, 644 (see p. 75) *Thomas Traherne*, poet, spiritual writer, 1674 DEL week 28	Gw	Romans 1.1–7 Psalm 98 Luke 11.29–32		Psalm 44 Ecclesiasticus 1.1–10 or Ezekiel 1.1–14 Mark 12.28–34	Psalms 47, 49 1 Kings 12.25—13.10 Acts 9.8–20
Tuesday 11 October *Ethelburga*, abbess, 675 *James the Deacon*, companion of Paulinus, 7th cent.	G	Romans 1.16–25 Psalm 19.1–4 Luke 11.37–41		Psalms 48, 52 Ecclesiasticus 1.11–end or Ezekiel 1.15—2.2 Mark 12.35–end	Psalm 50 1 Kings 13.11–end Acts 19.21–end
Wednesday 12 October *Wilfrid*, bishop, missionary, 709 (see p. 75) *Elizabeth Fry*, prison reformer, 1845 *Edith Cavell*, nurse, 1915	Gw	Romans 2.1–11 Psalm 62.1–8 Luke 11.42–46		Psalm 119.57–80 Ecclesiasticus 2 or Ezekiel 2.3—3.11 Mark 13.1–13	Psalms 59, 60 (67) 1 Kings 17 Acts 20.1–16
Thursday 13 October *Edward the Confessor*, king, 1066 (see p. 76)	Gw	Romans 3.21–30 Psalm 130 Luke 11.47–end		Psalms 56, 57 (63*) Ecclesiasticus 3.17–29 or Ezekiel 3.12–end Mark 13.14–23	Psalms 61, 62, 64 1 Kings 18.1–20 Acts 20.17–end
Friday 14 October	G	Romans 4.1–8 Psalm 32 Luke 12.1–7		Psalms 51, 54 Ecclesiasticus 4.11–28 or Ezekiel 8 Mark 13.24–31	Psalm 38 1 Kings 18.21–end Acts 21.1–16
Saturday 15 October *Teresa of Avila*, teacher of the faith, 1582 (see p. 73)	Gw	Romans 4.13, 16–18 Psalm 105.6–10, 41–44 Luke 12.8–12		Psalm 68 Ecclesiasticus 4.29—6.1 or Ezekiel 9 Mark 13.32–end	Psalms 65, 66 1 Kings 19 Acts 21.17–36

	Principal Service	3rd Service	2nd Service
Sunday 16 October 17th Sunday after Trinity Proper 24 G	Continuous: Exodus 33.12–end Psalm 99 Related: Isaiah 45.1–7 Psalm 96.1–9 [10–13] 1 Thessalonians 1.1–10 Matthew 22.15–22	Psalms 145, 149 Isaiah 54.1–7 Luke 13.31–35	Psalms 142 [143.1–11] Proverbs 4.1–18 1 John 3.16—4.6 HC Mark 10.35–45
	Holy Communion	**Morning Prayer**	**Evening Prayer**
Monday 17 October Ignatius, bishop, martyr, c.107 (see p. 72) DEL week 29 Gr	Romans 4.20–end Canticle: Benedictus 1–6 Luke 12.13–21	Psalm 71 Ecclesiasticus 6.14–end or Ezekiel 10.1–19 Mark 14.1–11	Psalms 72, 75 1 Kings 21 Acts 21.37—22.21 or: 1st EP of Luke the Evangelist: Psalm 33; Hosea 6.1–3; 2 Timothy 3.10–end
	Principal Service	**3rd Service**	**2nd Service**
Tuesday 18 October Luke the Evangelist R	Isaiah 35.3–6 or Acts 16.6–12a Psalm 147.1–7 2 Timothy 4.5–17 Luke 10.1–9	MP Psalms 145, 146 Isaiah 55 Luke 1.1–4	EP Psalm 103 Ecclesiasticus 38.1–14 or Isaiah 61.1–6 Colossians 4.7–end
	Holy Communion	**Morning Prayer**	**Evening Prayer**
Wednesday 19 October Henry Martyn, translator, missionary, 1812 (see p. 75) Gw	Romans 6.12–18 Psalm 124 Luke 12.39–48	Psalm 77 Ecclesiasticus 10.6–8, 12–24 or Ezekiel 12.1–16 Mark 14.26–42	Psalm 119.81–104 1 Kings 22.29–45 Acts 23.12–end
Thursday 20 October G	Romans 6.19–end Psalm 1 Luke 12.49–53	Psalm 78.1–39* Ecclesiasticus 11.7–28 or Ezekiel 12.17–end Mark 14.43–52	Psalm 78.40–end* 2 Kings 1.2–17 Acts 24.1–23
Friday 21 October G	Romans 7.18–end Psalm 119.33–40 Luke 12.54–end	Psalm 55 Ecclesiasticus 14.20—15.10 or Ezekiel 13.1–16 Mark 14.53–65	Psalm 69 2 Kings 2.1–18 Acts 24.24—25.12
Saturday 22 October G	Romans 8.1–11 Psalm 24.1–6 Luke 13.1–9	Psalms 76, 79 Ecclesiasticus 15.11–end or Ezekiel 14.1–11 Mark 14.66–end	Psalms 81, 84 2 Kings 4.1–37 Acts 25.13–end

Last after Trinity

	Principal Service	3rd Service	2nd Service
Sunday **23 October** **Last Sunday after Trinity** Proper 25 G	*Continuous:* Deuteronomy 34.1–12 Psalm 90.1–6, 13–17 [or 1–6] *Related:* Leviticus 19.1–2, 15–18 Psalm 1 1 Thessalonians 2.1–8 Matthew 22.34–end	Psalm 119.137–152 Isaiah 59.9–20 Luke 14.1–14	Psalm 119.89–104 Ecclesiastes 11, 12 2 Timothy 2.1–7 HC Mark 12.28–34

or, when the date of dedication of a church is not known, the Dedication Festival (W) may be celebrated today or on 2 October, or on a suitable date chosen locally (see p. 00).

	Principal Service	3rd Service	2nd Service
Or Sunday **23 October** **Bible Sunday** G	Nehemiah 8.1–4a [5–6] 8–12 Psalm 119.9–16 Colossians 3.12–17 Matthew 24.30–35	Psalm 119.137–152 Deuteronomy 17.14–15, 18–end John 5.36b–end	Psalm 119.89–104 Isaiah 55.1–11 Luke 4.14–30

	Holy Communion	Morning Prayer	Evening Prayer
Monday 24 October DEL week 30 G	Romans 8.12–17 Psalm 68.1–6, 19 Luke 13.10–17	Psalms 80, 82 Ecclesiasticus 16.17–end or Ezekiel 14.12–end Mark 15.1–15	Psalms 85, 86 2 Kings 5 Acts 26.1–23
Tuesday 25 October *Crispin and Crispinian, martyrs, c.287* G	Romans 8.18–25 Psalm 126 Luke 13.18–21	Psalms 87, **89.1–18** Ecclesiasticus 17.1–24 or Ezekiel 18.1–20 Mark 15.16–32	Psalm **89.19–end** 2 Kings 6.1–23 Acts 26.24–end
Wednesday 26 October Gw Alfred, king, scholar, 899 (see p. 76) *Cedd, abbot, bishop, 664*	Romans 8.26–30 Psalm 13 Luke 13.22–30	Psalm **119.105–128** Ecclesiasticus 18.1–14 or Ezekiel 18.21–32 Mark 15.33–41	Psalms **91**, 93 2 Kings 9.1–16 Acts 27.1–26
Thursday 27 October G	Romans 8.31–end Psalm 109.20–26, 29–30 Luke 13.31–end	Psalms 90, **92** Ecclesiasticus 19.4–17 or Ezekiel 20.1–20 Mark 15.42–end	Psalm **94** 2 Kings 9.17–end Acts 27.27–end *or:* 1st EP of Simon and Jude, Apostles: Psalms 124, 125, 126; Deuteronomy 32.1–4; John 14.15–26

	Principal Service	3rd Service	2nd Service
Friday 28 October *R* Simon and Jude, Apostles	Isaiah 28.14–16 Psalm 119.89–96 Ephesians 2.19–end John 15.17–end	MP Psalms 116, 117 Wisdom 5.1–16 or Isaiah 45.18–end Luke 6.12–16	EP Psalm 119.1–16 1 Maccabees 2.42–66 or Jeremiah 3.11–18 Jude vv1–4, 17–end
	Holy Communion	Morning Prayer	Evening Prayer
Saturday 29 October *Gr* James Hannington, bishop, martyr, 1885 (see p. 72)	Romans 11.1–2, 11–12, 25–29 Psalm 94.14–19 Luke 14.1, 7–11	Psalms 96, **97**, 100 Ecclesiasticus 21.1–17 or Ezekiel 24.15–end Mark 16.9–end	Psalm 104 2 Kings 17.1–23 Acts 28.17–end *or where All Saints' Day is celebrated on* *Sunday 30 October only:* **1st EP of All Saints' Day:** Psalms 1, 5; Ecclesiasticus 44.1–15 or Isaiah 40.27–end; Revelation 19.6–10

65

4 before Advent / All Saints' Day

All Saints' Day is celebrated either on Tuesday 1 November or on Sunday 30 October; if the latter, there may be a supplementary celebration on 1 November.

Where All Saints' Day is celebrated on Tuesday 1 November:

	Principal Service	3rd Service	2nd Service
Sunday **30 October** **4th Sunday before Advent** G	Micah 3.5–end Psalm 43 [or Psalm 107.1–9] 1 Thessalonians 2.9–13 Matthew 24.1–14	Psalm 33 Isaiah 66.20–23 Ephesians 1.11–end	Psalms 111, 117 Daniel 7.1–18 Luke 6.17–31

Where All Saints' Day is celebrated on Sunday 30 October only:

	Principal Service	3rd Service	2nd Service
Or Sunday **30 October** All Saints' Day Gold or W	Revelation 7.9–end Psalm 34.1–10 1 John 3.1–3 Matthew 5.1–12	MP Psalms 15, 84, 149 Isaiah 35 Luke 9.18–27	EP Psalms 148, 150 Isaiah 65.17–end Hebrews 11.32—12.2

	Holy Communion	Morning Prayer	Evening Prayer
Monday **31 October** *Martin Luther, reformer, 1546* DEL week 31 G	Romans 11.29–end Psalm 69.31–37 Luke 14.12–14	Psalms **2**, 146 or **98**, 99, 101 Isaiah 1.1–20 Matthew 1.18–end	Psalms **92**, 96, 97 or **105*** (or 103) Daniel 1 Revelation 1 *or where All Saints' Day is celebrated on Tuesday 1 November only:* **1st EP of All Saints' Day:** Psalms 1, 5; Ecclesiasticus 44.1–15 or Isaiah 40.27–end; Revelation 19.6–10

	Principal Service	Morning Prayer	Evening Prayer
Tuesday **1 November** All Saints' Day Gold or W	Revelation 7.9–end Psalm 34.1–10 1 John 3.1–3 Matthew 5.1–12	MP Psalms 15, 84, 149 Isaiah 35 Luke 9.18–27	EP Psalms 148, 150 Isaiah 65.17–end Hebrews 11.32—12.2

Where All Saints' Day is celebrated on Sunday 30 October only:

	Principal Service	3rd Service	2nd Service
Or Tuesday **1 November** R/G	Romans 12.5–16 Psalm 131 Luke 14.15–24	Psalms **5**, 147.1–12 or **106*** (or 103) Isaiah 1.21–end Matthew 2.1–15	Psalms 98, 99, **100** or **107*** Daniel 2.1–24 Revelation 2.1–11

Where All Saints' Day is celebrated on Tuesday 1 November in addition to Sunday 30 October:

	Principal Service	3rd Service	2nd Service
Or Tuesday **1 November** All Saints' Day Gold or W	Isaiah 56.3–8 or 2 Esdras 2.42–end Psalm 33.1–5 Hebrews 12.18–24 Matthew 5.1–12	Psalms 111, 112, 117 Wisdom 5.1–16 or Jeremiah 31.31–34 2 Corinthians 4.5–12	Psalm 145 Isaiah 66.20–23 Colossians 1.9–14

Wednesday **2 November** Rp/Gp Commemoration of the Faithful Departed (All Souls' Day)	Romans 13.8–10 Psalm 112 Luke 14.25–33 *Lesser Festival eucharistic lectionary:* Lamentations 3.17–26, 31–33 or Wisdom 3.1–9; Psalm 23 or 27.1–6, 16–end Romans 5.5–11 or 1 Peter 1.3–9; John 5.19–25 or John 6.37–40	Psalms **9**, 147.13–end or 110, **111**, 112 Isaiah 2.1–11 Matthew 2.16–end	Psalms 111, **112**, 116 or **119.129–152** Daniel 2.25–end Revelation 2.12–end
Thursday **3 November** Rw/Gw Richard Hooker, priest, teacher of the faith, 1600 (see p.73) *Martin of Porres, friar, 1639*	Romans 14.7–12 Psalm 27.14–end Luke 15.1–10	Psalms 11, **15**, 148 or 113, **115** Isaiah 2.12–end Matthew 3	Psalms 118 or 114, **116**, 117 Daniel 3.1–18 Revelation 3.1–13
Friday **4 November** R/G	Romans 15.14–21 Psalm 98 Luke 16.1–8	Psalms **16**, 149 or **139** Isaiah 3.1–15 Matthew 4.1–11	Psalms 137, 138, **143** or **130**, 131, 137 Daniel 3.19–end Revelation 3.14–end
Saturday **5 November** R/G	Romans 16.3–9, 16, 22–end Psalm 145.1–7 Luke 16.9–15	Psalms **18.31–end**, 150 or 120, 121, 122 Isaiah 4.2—5.7 Matthew 4.12–22	Psalm **145** or 118 Daniel 4.1–18 Revelation 4

		Principal Service	3rd Service	2nd Service
			Morning Prayer	Evening Prayer
Sunday	**6 November** *R/G* **3rd Sunday before Advent**	Wisdom of Solomon 6.12–16 or Amos 5.18–24 Canticle: Wisdom of Solomon 6.17–20 or Psalm 70 1 Thessalonians 4.13–end Matthew 25.1–13	Psalm 91 Deuteronomy 17.14–end 1 Timothy 2.1–7	Psalms [20] 82 Judges 7.2–22 John 15.9–17
Monday	**7 November** *Rw/Gw* Willibrord, bishop, 739 (see p. 75) DEL week 32	*Holy Communion* Wisdom 1.1–7 or Titus 1.1–9 Psalm 139.1–9 or 24.1–6 Luke 17.1–6	Psalms **19**, **20** or 123, 124, 125, **126** Isaiah 5.8–24 Matthew 4.23—5.12	Psalms **34** or **127**, 128, 129 Daniel 4.19–end Revelation 5
Tuesday	**8 November** *Rw/Gw* Saints and martyrs of England	Wisdom 2.23—3.9 or Titus 2.1–8, 11–14 Psalm 34.1–6 or 37.3–5, 30–32 Luke 17.7–10 *Lesser Festival eucharistic lectionary:* Isaiah 61.4–9 or Ecclesiasticus 44.1–15; Psalm 15; Revelation 19.5–10; John 17.18–23	Psalms **21**, 24 or **132**, 133 Isaiah 5.25–end Matthew 5.13–20	Psalms 36, **40** or (134), **135** Daniel 5.1–12 Revelation 6
Wednesday	**9 November** *R/G* *Margery Kempe, mystic, c.1440*	Wisdom 6.1–11 or Titus 3.1–7 Psalm 82 or 23 Luke 17.11–19	Psalms **23**, 25 or **119.153–end** Isaiah 6 Matthew 5.21–37	Psalm **37** or **136** Daniel 5.13–end Revelation 7.1–4, 9–end
Thursday	**10 November** *Rw/Gw* Leo the Great, bishop, teacher of the faith, 461 (see p. 73)	Wisdom 7.22—8.1 or Philemon vv 7–20 Psalm 119.89–96 or 146.4–end Luke 17.20–25	Psalms **26**, 27 or **143**, 146 Isaiah 7.1–17 Matthew 5.38–end	Psalms 42, **43** or **138**, 140, 141 Daniel 6 Revelation 8
Friday	**11 November** *Rw/Gw* Martin, bishop, c.397 (see p. 74)	Wisdom 13.1–9 or 2 John vv 4–9 Psalm 19.1–4 or 119.1–8 Luke 17.26–end	Psalms 28, **32** or 142, **144** Isaiah 8.1–15 Matthew 6.1–18	Psalm **31** or **145** Daniel 7.1–14 Revelation 9.1–12
Saturday	**12 November** *R/G*	Wisdom 18.14–16, 19.6–9 or 3 John vv 5–8 Psalm 105.1–5, 35–42 or 112 Luke 18.1–8	Psalm **33** or **147** Isaiah 8.16—9.7 Matthew 6.19–end	Psalms 84, **86** or **148**, 149, 150 Daniel 7.15–end Revelation 9.13–end

		Principal Service	3rd Service	2nd Service
Sunday	**13 November** *R/G* **2nd Sunday before Advent** *Remembrance Sunday*	Zephaniah 1.7, 12–end Psalm 90.1–8 [9–11] 12 [or 1–8] 1 Thessalonians 5.1–11 Matthew 25.14–30	Psalm 98 Daniel 10.19–end Revelation 4	Psalm 89.19–37 [or 19–29] 1 Kings 1.15–40 [or 1–40] Revelation 1.4–18 HC Luke 9.1–6
		Holy Communion	*Morning Prayer*	*Evening Prayer*
Monday	**14 November** *R/G* *Samuel Seabury, bishop, 1796* DEL week 33	1 Maccabees 1.10–15, 41–43, 54–57, 62–64 or Revelation 1.1–4, 2.1–5 Psalm 79.1–5 or 1 Luke 18.35–end	Psalms 46, **47** or 1, 2, 3 Isaiah 9.8–10.4 Matthew 7.1–12	Psalms 70, **71** or **4**, 7 Daniel 8.1–14 Revelation 10
Tuesday	**15 November** *R/G*	2 Maccabees 6.18–end or Revelation 3.1–6, 14–31 Psalm 11 or 15 Luke 19.1–10	Psalms 48, **52** or 5, 6 (8) Isaiah 10.5–19 Matthew 7.13–end	Psalms **67**, 72 or **9**, 10* Daniel 8.15–end Revelation 11.1–14
Wednesday	**16 November** *Rw/Gw* *Margaret, queen, philanthropist, 1093* (see p. 76) *Edmund Rich, archbishop, 1240*	2 Maccabees 7.1, 20–31 or Revelation 4 Psalm 116.10–end or 150 Luke 19.11–28	Psalms **56**, 57 or **119.1–32** Isaiah 10.20–32 Matthew 8.1–13	Psalms **73** or **11**, 12, 13 Daniel 9.1–19 Revelation 11.15–end
Thursday	**17 November** *Rw/Gw* *Hugh, bishop, 1200 (see p. 74)*	1 Maccabees 2.15–29 or Revelation 5.1–10 Psalm 129 or 149.1–5 Luke 19.41–44	Psalms 61, **62** or 14, **15**, 16 Isaiah 10.33—11.9 Matthew 8.14–22	Psalms 74, **76** or **18*** Daniel 9.20–end Revelation 12
Friday	**18 November** *Rw/Gw* *Elizabeth, princess, philanthropist, 1231* (see p. 76)	1 Maccabees 4.36–37, 52–59 or Revelation 10.8–11 Psalm 122 or 119.65–72 Luke 19.45–48	Psalms **63**, 65 or 17, **19** Isaiah 11.10–end of 12 Matthew 8.23–end	Psalm 77 or **22** Daniel 10.1—11.1 Revelation 13.1–10
Saturday	**19 November** *Rw/Gw* *Hilda, abbess, 680 (see p. 75)* *Mechtild, béguine, mystic, 1280*	1 Maccabees 6.1–13 or Revelation 11.4–12 Psalm 124 or 144.1–9 Luke 20.27–40	Psalms **78.1–39** or 20, 21, **23** Isaiah 13.1–13 Matthew 9.1–17	Psalms **78.40–end** or **24**, 25 Daniel 12 Revelation 13.11–end or: 1st EP of Christ the King: Psalms 99, 100; Isaiah 10.33—11.9; 1 Timothy 6.11–16

Christ the King / Sunday next before Advent

		Principal Service	3rd Service	2nd Service
Sunday	**20 November** *R/W* Christ the King Sunday next before Advent	Ezekiel 34.11–16, 20–24 Psalm 95.1–7 Ephesians 1.15–end Matthew 25.31–end	MP Psalms 29, 110 Isaiah 4.2—5.7 Luke 19.29–38	EP Psalms 93 [97] 2 Samuel 23.1–7 or 1 Maccabees 2.15–29 Matthew 28.16–end
		Holy Communion	**Morning Prayer**	**Evening Prayer**
Monday	**21 November** *R/G* DEL week 34	Daniel 1.1–6, 8–20 *Canticle:* Bless the Lord Luke 21.1–4	Psalms 92, **96** or 27, **30** Isaiah 14.3–20 Matthew 9.18–34	Psalms **80**, 81 or 26, **28**, 29 Isaiah 40.1–11 Revelation 14.1–13
Tuesday	**22 November** *R/G* *Cecilia, martyr, c.230*	Daniel 2.31–45 *Canticle:* Benedicite 1–3 Luke 21.5–11	Psalms **97**, 98, 100 or 32, **36** Isaiah 17 Matthew 9.35—10.15	Psalms 99, **101** or **33** Isaiah 40.12–26 Revelation 14.14—end of 15
Wednesday	**23 November** *R/Gr* Clement, bishop, martyr, c.100 (see p. 72)	Daniel 5.1–6, 13–14, 16–17, 23–28 *Canticle:* Benedicite 4–5 Luke 21.12–19	Psalms 110, 111, **112** or **34** Isaiah 19 Matthew 10.16–33	Psalms 121, **122**, 123, 124 or **119.33–56** Isaiah 40.27—41.7 Revelation 16.1–11
Thursday	**24 November** *R/G*	Daniel 6.12–end *Canticle:* Benedicite 6–8a Luke 21.20–28	Psalms **125**, 126, 127, 128 or **37*** Isaiah 21.1–12 Matthew 10.34—11.1	Psalms 131, 132, **133** or 39, **40** Isaiah 41.8–20 Revelation 16.12–end
Friday	**25 November** *R/G* Catherine, martyr, 4th cent. Isaac Watts, hymn writer, 1748	Daniel 7.2–14 *Canticle:* Benedicite 8b–10a Luke 21.29–33	Psalm **139** or **31** Isaiah 22.1–14 Matthew 11.2–19	Psalms **146**, 147 or **35** Isaiah 41.21—42.9 Revelation 17
Saturday	**26 November** *R/G*	Daniel 7.15–27 *Canticle:* Benedicite 10b–end Luke 21.34–36	Psalms **145** or 41, **42**, 43 Isaiah 24 Matthew 11.20–end	Psalms 148, 149, **150** or 45, **46** Isaiah 42.10–17 Revelation 18

¶ *Collects and Post Communions*

All the contemporary language Collects and Post Communions, including the Additional Collects, may be found in *Common Worship: Collects and Post Communions* (Church House Publishing: London, 2004). The Additional Collects are also published separately.

The contemporary language Collects and Post Communions, apart from the Additional Collects, appear in the other Common Worship volumes as follows:

¶ President's edition: all Collects and Post Communions;
¶ *Daily Prayer:* all Collects;
¶ main volume: Collects and Post Communions for Sundays, Principal Feasts and Holy Days, and Festivals;
¶ *Festivals:* Collects and Post Communions for Festivals, Lesser Festivals, Common of the Saints and Special Occasions.

The traditional-language Collects and Post Communions all appear in the president's edition. They appear in other publications as follows:

¶ main volume: Collects and Post Communions for Sundays, Principal Feasts and Holy Days, and Festivals;
¶ separate booklet: Collects and Post Communions for Lesser Festivals, Common of the Saints and Special Occasions.

¶ *Lectionary for Dedication Festival*

If date not known, observe on the first Sunday in October or Last Sunday after Trinity.

Evening Prayer on the Eve	Psalm 24 2 Chronicles 7.11–16 John 4.19–29

Dedication Festival — *Gold or White*

	Principal Service	3rd Service	2nd Service	Psalmody
Year A	1 Kings 8.22–30 or Revelation 21.9–14 Psalm 122 Hebrews 12.18–24 Matthew 21.12–16	Haggai 2.6–9 Hebrews 10.19–25	Jeremiah 7.1–11 1 Corinthians 3.9–17 HC Luke 19.1–10	MP 48, 150 EP 132
Year B	Genesis 28.11–18 or Revelation 21.9–14 Psalm 122 1 Peter 2.1–10 John 10.22–29	Haggai 2.6–9 Hebrews 10.19–25	Jeremiah 7.1–11 Luke 19.1–10	MP 48, 150 EP 132
Year C	1 Chronicles 29.6–19 Psalm 122 Ephesians 2.19–22 John 2.13–22	Haggai 2.6–9 Hebrews 10.19–25	Jeremiah 7.1–11 Luke 19.1–10	MP 48, 150 EP 132

The Blessed Virgin Mary

Genesis 3.8–15, 20; Isaiah 7.10–14; Micah 5.1–4
Psalms 45.10–17; 113; 131
Acts 1.12–14; Romans 8.18–30; Galatians 4.4–7
Luke 1.26–38; *or* 1.39–47; John 19.25–27

Martyrs

2 Chronicles 24.17–21; Isaiah 43.1–7; Jeremiah 11.18–20; Wisdom 4.10–15
Psalms 3; 11; 31.1–5; 44.18–24; 126
Romans 8.35–end; 2 Corinthians 4.7–15; 2 Timothy 2.3–7 [8–13]; Hebrews 11.32–end;
    1 Peter 4.12–end; Revelation 12.10–12a
Matthew 10.16–22; *or* 10.28–39; *or* 16.24–26; John 12.24–26; *or* 15.18–21

Agnes (21 Jan): *also* Revelation 7.13–end
Alban (22 June): *especially* 2 Timothy 2.3–13; John 12.24–26
Alphege (19 Apr): *also* Hebrews 5.1–4
Boniface (5 June): *also* Acts 20.24–28
Charles (30 Jan): *also* Ecclesiasticus 2.12–end; 1 Timothy 6.12–16
Clement (23 Nov): *also* Philippians 3.17—4.3; Matthew 16.13–19
Cyprian (15 Sept): *especially* 1 Peter 4.12–end; *also* Matthew 18.18–22
Edmund (20 Nov): *also* Proverbs 20.28; 21.1–4, 7
Ignatius (17 Oct): *also* Philippians 3.7–12; John 6.52–58
James Hannington (29 Oct): *especially* Matthew 10.28–39
Janani Luwum (17 Feb): *also* Ecclesiasticus 4.20–28; John 12.24–32
John Coleridge Patteson (20 Sept): *especially* 2 Chronicles 24.17–21; *also* Acts 7.55–end
Justin (1 June): *especially* John 15.18–21; *also* 1 Maccabees 2.15–22; 1 Corinthians 1.18–25
Laurence (10 Aug): *also* 2 Corinthians 9.6–10
Lucy (13 Dec): *also* Wisdom 3.1–7; 2 Corinthians 4.6–15
Oswald (5 Aug): *especially* 1 Peter 4.12–end; John 16.29–end
Perpetua, Felicity and comps (7 Mar): *especially* Revelation 12.10–12a; *also* Wisdom 3.1–7
Polycarp (23 Feb): *also* Revelation 2.8–11
Thomas Becket (29 Dec *or* 7 Jul): *especially* Matthew 10.28–33; *also* Ecclesiasticus 51.1–8
William Tyndale (6 Oct): *also* Proverbs 8.4–11; 2 Timothy 3.12–end

Teachers of the Faith and Spiritual Writers

I Kings 3.[6–10] 11–14; Proverbs 4.1–9; Wisdom 7.7–10, 15–16; Ecclesiasticus 39.1–10
Psalms 19.7–10; 34.11–17; 37.31–35; 119.89–96; 119.97–104
I Corinthians 1.18–25; or 2.1–10; or 2.9–end; Ephesians 3.8–12; 2 Timothy 4.1–8;
    Titus 2.1–8
Matthew 5.13–19; or 13.52–end; or 23.8–12; Mark 4.1–9; John 16.12–15

Ambrose (7 Dec): *also* Isaiah 41.9b–13; Luke 22.24–30
Anselm (21 Apr): *also* Wisdom 9.13–end; Romans 5.8–11
Athanasius (2 May): *also* Ecclesiasticus 4.20–28; *also* Matthew 10.24–27
Augustine of Hippo (28 Aug): *especially* Ecclesiasticus 39.1–10; *also* Romans 13.11–13
Basil and Gregory (2 Jan): *especially* 2 Timothy 4.1–8; Matthew 5.13–19
Bernard (20 Aug): *especially* Revelation 19.5–9
Catherine of Siena (29 Apr): *also* Proverbs 8.1, 6–11; John 17.12–end
Francis de Sales (24 Jan): *also* Proverbs 3.13–18; John 3.17–21
Gregory the Great (3 Sept): *also* I Thessalonians 2.3–8
Gregory of Nyssa and Macrina (19 July): *especially* I Corinthians 2.9–13;
    also Wisdom 9.13–17
Hilary (13 Jan): *also* I John 2.18–25; John 8.25–32
Irenaeus (28 June): *also* 2 Peter 1.16–end
Jeremy Taylor (13 Aug): *also* Titus 2.7–8, 11–14
John Bunyan (30 Aug): *also* Hebrews 12.1–2; Luke 21.21, 34–36
John Chrysostom (13 Sept): *especially* Matthew 5.13–19; *also* Jeremiah 1.4–10
John of the Cross (14 Dec): *especially* I Corinthians 2.1–10; *also* John 14.18–23
Leo (10 Nov): *also* I Peter 5.1–11
Richard Hooker (3 Nov): *especially* John 16.12–15; *also* Ecclesiasticus 44.10–15
Teresa of Avila (15 Oct): *also* Romans 8.22–27
Thomas Aquinas (28 Jan): *especially* Wisdom 7.7–10, 15–16; I Corinthians 2.9–end;
    John 16.12–15
William Law (10 Apr): *especially* I Corinthians 2.9–end; *also* Matthew 17.1–9

Bishops and Other Pastors

I Samuel 16.1, 6–13; Isaiah 6.1–8; Jeremiah 1.4–10; Ezekiel 3.16–21; Malachi 2.5–7
Psalms 1; 15; 16.5–end; 96; 110
Acts 20.28–35; I Corinthians 4.1–5; 2 Corinthians 4.1–10 [or 1–2, 5–7];
   or 5.14–20; I Peter 5.1–4
Matthew 11.25–end; or 24.42–46; John 10.11–16; or 15.9–17; or 21.15–17

Augustine of Canterbury (26 May): *also* I Thessalonians 2.2*b*–8; Matthew 13.31–33
Charles Simeon (13 Nov): *especially* Malachi 2.5–7; *also* Colossians 1.3–8; Luke 8.4–8
David (1 Mar): *also* 2 Samuel 23.1–4; Psalm 89.19–22, 24
Dunstan (19 May): *especially* Matthew 24.42–46; *also* Exodus 31.1–5
Edward King (8 Mar): *also* Hebrews 13.1–8
George Herbert (27 Feb): *especially* Malachi 2.5–7; Matthew 11.25–end;
   also Revelation 19.5–9
Hugh (17 Nov): *also* I Timothy 6.11–16
John Keble (14 July): *also* Lamentations 3.19–26; Matthew 5.1–8
John and Charles Wesley (24 May): *also* Ephesians 5.15–20
Lancelot Andrewes (25 Sept): *especially* Isaiah 6.1–8
Martin of Tours (11 Nov): *also* I Thessalonians 5.1–11; Matthew 25.34–40
Nicholas (6 Dec): *also* Isaiah 61.1–3; I Timothy 6.6–11; Mark 10.13–16
Richard (16 June): *also* John 21.15–19
Swithun (15 July): *also* James 5.7–11, 13–18
Thomas Ken (8 June): *especially* 2 Corinthians 4.1–10 [or 1–2, 5–7]; Matthew 24.42–46
Wulfstan (19 Jan): *especially* Matthew 24.42–46

Members of Religious Communities

1 Kings 19.9–18; Proverbs 10.27–end; Song of Solomon 8.6–7; Isaiah 61.10—62.5;
    Hosea 2.14–15, 19–20
Psalms 34.1–8; 112.1–9; 119.57–64; 123; 131
Acts 4.32–35; 2 Corinthians 10.17—11.2; Philippians 3.7–14; 1 John 2.15–17;
    Revelation 19.1, 5–9
Matthew 11.25–end; *or* 19.3–12; *or* 19.23–end; Luke 9.57–end; *or* 12.32–37

Aelred (12 Jan): *also* Ecclesiasticus 15.1–6
Alcuin (20 May): *also* Colossians 3.12–16; John 4.19–24
Antony (17 Jan): *especially* Philippians 3.7–14, *also* Matthew 19.16–26
Bede (25 May): *also* Ecclesiasticus 39.1–10
Benedict (11 July): *also* 1 Corinthians 3.10–11; Luke 18.18–22
Clare (11 Aug): *especially* Song of Solomon 8.6–7
Dominic (8 Aug): *also* Ecclesiasticus 39.1–10
Etheldreda (23 June): *also* Matthew 25.1–13
Francis of Assisi (4 Oct): *also* Galatians 6.14–end; Luke 12.22–34
Hilda (19 Nov): *especially* Isaiah 61.10—62.5
Hildegard (17 Sept): *also* 1 Corinthians 2.9–13; Luke 10.21–24
Julian of Norwich (8 May): *also* 1 Corinthians 13.8–end; Matthew 5.13–16
Vincent de Paul (27 Sept): *also* 1 Corinthians 1.25–end; Matthew 25.34–40

Missionaries

Isaiah 52.7–10; *or* 61.1–3*a*; Ezekiel 34.11–16; Jonah 3.1–5
Psalms 67; *or* 87; *or* 97; *or* 100; *or* 117
Acts 2.14, 22–36; *or* 13.46–49; *or* 16.6–10; *or* 26.19–23; Romans 15.17–21;
    2 Corinthians 5.11—6.2
Matthew 9.35–end; *or* 28.16–end; Mark 16.15–20; Luke 5.1–11; *or* 10.1–9

Aidan (31 Aug): *also* 1 Corinthians 9.16–19
Anskar (3 Feb): *especially* Isaiah 52.7–10; *also* Romans 10.11–15
Chad (2 Mar *or* 26 Oct): *also* 1 Timothy 6.11*b*–16
Columba (9 June): *also* Titus 2.11–end
Cuthbert (20 Mar *or* 4 Sept): *especially* Ezekiel 34.11–16; *also* Matthew 18.12–14
Cyril and Methodius (14 Feb): *especially* Isaiah 52.7–10; *also* Romans 10.11–15
Henry Martyn (19 Oct): *especially* Mark 16.15–end; *also* Isaiah 55.6–11
Ninian (16 Sept): *especially* Acts 13.46–49; Mark 16.15–end
Patrick (17 Mar): *also* Psalm 91.1–4, 13–16; Luke 10.1–12, 17–20
Paulinus (10 Oct): *especially* Matthew 28.16–end
Wilfrid (12 Oct): *especially* Luke 5.1–11; *also* 1 Corinthians 1.18–25
Willibrord (7 Nov): *especially* Isaiah 52.7–10; Matthew 28.16–end

Any Saint

General

Genesis 12.1–4; Proverbs 8.1–11; Micah 6.6–8; Ecclesiasticus 2.7–13 [14–end]
Psalms 32; 33.1–5; 119.1–8; 139.1–4 [5–12]; 145.8–14
Ephesians 3.14–19; or 6.11–18; Hebrews 13.7–8, 15–16; James 2.14–17;
    I John 4.7–16; Revelation 21.[1–4] 5–7
Matthew 19.16–21; or 25.1–13; or 25.14–30; John 15.1–8; or 17.20–end

Christian rulers

I Samuel 16.1–13a; I Kings 3.3–14
Psalms 72.1–7; 99
I Timothy 2.1–6
Mark 10.42–45; Luke 14.27–33

Alfred the Great (26 Oct): *also* 2 Samuel 23.1–5; John 18.33–37
Edward the Confessor (13 Oct): *also* 2 Samuel 23.1–5; I John 4.13–16
Margaret of Scotland (16 Nov): *also* Proverbs 31.10–12, 20, 26–end;
    I Corinthians 12.13—13.3; Matthew 25.34–end

Those working for the poor and underprivileged

Isaiah 58.6–11
Psalms 82; 146.5–10
Hebrews 13.1–3; I John 3.14–18
Matthew 5.1–12; or 25.31–end

Elizabeth of Hungary (18 Nov): *especially* Matthew 25.31–end; *also* Proverbs 31.10–end
Josephine Butler (30 May): *especially* Isaiah 58.6–11; *also* I John 3.18–23; Matthew 9.10–13
William Wilberforce (30 July): *also* Job 31.16–23; Galatians 3.26–end, 4.6–7; Luke 4.16–21

Men and women of learning

Proverbs 8.22–31; Ecclesiasticus 44.1–15
Psalms 36.5–10; 49.1–4
Philippians 4.7–8
Matthew 13.44–46, 52; John 7.14–18

Those whose holiness was revealed in marriage and family life

Proverbs 31.10–13, 19–20, 30–end; Tobit 8.4–7
Psalms 127; 128
I Peter 3.1–9
Mark 3.31–end; Luke 10.38–end

Mary Sumner (9 Aug): *also* Hebrews 13.1–5
Monica (27 Aug): *also* Ecclesiasticus 26.1–3, 13–16

The Guidance of the Holy Spirit

Proverbs 24.3–7; Isaiah 30.15–21; Wisdom 9.13–17
Psalms 25.1–9; 104.26–33; 143.8–10
Acts 15.23–29; Romans 8.22–27; 1 Corinthians 12.4–13
Luke 14.27–33; John 14.23–26; *or* 16.13–15

Rogation Days
(30 May–1 June in 2011)

Deuteronomy 8.1–10; 1 Kings 8.35–40; Job 28.1–11
Psalms 104.21–30; 107.1–9; 121
Philippians 4.4–7; 2 Thessalonians 3.6–13; 1 John 5.12–15
Matthew 6.1–15; Mark 11.22–24; Luke 11.5–13

Harvest Thanksgiving

Year A	Year B	Year C
Deuteronomy 8.7–18 *or* 28.1–14	Joel 2.21–27	Deuteronomy 26.1–11
Psalm 65	Psalm 126	Psalm 100
2 Corinthians 9.6–end	1 Timothy 2.1–7 *or* 6.6–10	Philippians 4.4–9
Luke 12.16–30 *or* 17.11–19	Matthew 6.25–33	*or* Revelation 14.14–18
		John 6.25–35

Mission and Evangelism

Isaiah 49.1–6; *or* 52.7–10; Micah 4.1–5
Psalms 2; 46; 67
Acts 17.10–end; 2 Corinthians 5.14—6.2; Ephesians 2.13–end
Matthew 5.13–16; *or* 28.16–end; John 17.20–end

The Unity of the Church

Jeremiah 33.6–9*a*; Ezekiel 36.23–28; Zephaniah 3.16–end
Psalms 100; 122; 133
Ephesians 4.1–6; Colossians 3.9–17; 1 John 4.9–15
Matthew 18.19–22; John 11.45–52; *or* 17.11*b*–23

The Peace of the World

Isaiah 9.1–6; *or* 57.15–19; Micah 4.1–5
Psalms 40.14–17; 72.1–7; 85.8–13
Philippians 4.6–9; 1 Timothy 2.1–6; James 3.13–18
Matthew 5.43–end; John 14.23–29; *or* 15.9–17

Social Justice and Responsibility

Isaiah 32.15–end; Amos 5.21–24; or 8.4–7; Acts 5.1–11
Psalms 31.21–24; 85.1–7; 146.5–10
Colossians 3.12–15; James 2.1–4
Matthew 5.1–12; or 25.31–end; Luke 16.19–end

Ministry, including Ember Days
(See page 6)

Numbers 11.16–17, 24–29; or 27.15–end; 1 Samuel 16.1–13a; Isaiah 6.1–8;
    or 61.1–3; Jeremiah 1.4–10
Psalms 40.8–13; 84.8–12; 89.19–25; 101.1–5, 7; 122
Acts 20.28–35; 1 Corinthians 3.3–11; Ephesians 4.4–16; Philippians 3.7–14
Luke 4.16–21; or 12.35–43; or 22.24–27; John 4.31–38; or 15.5–17

In Time of Trouble

Genesis 9.8–17; Job 1.13–end; Isaiah 38.6–11
Psalms 86.1–7; 107.4–15; 142.1–7
Romans 3.21–26; Romans 8.18–25; 2 Corinthians 8.1–5, 9
Mark 4.35–end; Luke 12.1–7; John 16.31–end

For the Sovereign

Joshua 1.1–9; Proverbs 8.1–16
Psalms 20; 101; 121
Romans 13.1–10; Revelation 21.22—22.4
Matthew 22.16–22; Luke 22.24–30

The anniversary of HM The Queen's accession is 6 February.

Psalms in the Course of a Month

The following provision may be used for a monthly cycle of psalmody in place of the psalms provided in the tables in this booklet. It is based on the provision in The Book of Common Prayer.

	Morning Prayer	Evening Prayer
1	1—5	6—8
2	9—11	12—14
3	15—17	18
4	19—21	22—23
5	24—26	27—29
6	30—31	32—34
7	35—36	37
8	38—40	41—43
9	44—46	47—49
10	50—52	53—55
11	56—58	59—61
12	62—64	65—67
13	68	69—70
14	71—72	73—74
15	75—77	78
16	79—81	82—85
17	86—88	89
18	90—92	93—94
19	95—97	98—101
20	102—103	104
21	105	106
22	107	108—109
23	110—112	113—115
24	116—118	119.1–32
25	119.33–72	119.73–96
26	119.97—144	119.145–176
27	120—125	126—131
28	132—135	136—138
29	139—140	141—143
30	144—146	147—150

In February the psalms are read only to the 28th or 29th day of the month.

In January, March, May, July, August, October and December, all of which have 31 days, the same psalms are read on the last day of the month (being an ordinary weekday) which were read the day before, or else the psalms of the monthly course omitted on one of the Sundays in that month.

Concise Calendar November 2011 – December 2012

Advent 2011 to the eve of Advent 2012: Year B (Daily Eucharistic Lectionary Year 2)

November 2011

		3bAdv	2bAdv	ChrK	Adv1
Sunday					
Monday		7	14	21	28
Tuesday	AllSS	8	15	22	29
Wednesday	2	9	16	23	30
Thursday	3	10	17	24	
Friday	4	11	18	25	
Saturday	5	12	19	26	

December 2011

		Adv2	Adv3	Adv4	Chr
Sunday					
Monday		5	12	19	26
Tuesday		6	13	20	27
Wednesday		7	14	21	28
Thursday	1	8	15	22	29
Friday	2	9	16	23	30
Saturday	3	10	17	24	31

January 2012

	Chr1	Bapt	Ep2	Ep3	Ep4
Sunday					
Monday	2	9	16	23	30
Tuesday	3	10	17	24	31
Wednesday	4	11	18	25	
Thursday	5	12	19	26	
Friday	Ep	13	20	27	
Saturday	7	14	21	28	

February

		3bLnt	2bLnt	SbLnt	Lnt1
Sunday					
Monday		6	13	20	27
Tuesday		7	14	21	28
Wednesday	1	8	15	Ash	29
Thursday	Pres	9	16	23	
Friday	3	10	17	24	
Saturday	4	11	18	25	

March

		Lnt2	Lnt3	Lnt4	Lnt5
Sunday					
Monday		5	12	19	Ann
Tuesday		6	13	20	27
Wednesday		7	14	21	28
Thursday	1	8	15	22	29
Friday	2	9	16	23	30
Saturday	3	10	17	24	31

April

	PmS	Est	Est2	Est3	Est4
Sunday					
Monday	2	9	16	23	30
Tuesday	3	10	17	24	
Wednesday	4	11	18	25	
Thursday	MTh	12	19	26	
Friday	GFr	13	20	27	
Saturday	7	14	21	28	

May

		Est5	Est6	Est7	Pent
Sunday					
Monday		7	14	21	28
Tuesday	1	8	15	22	29
Wednesday	2	9	16	23	30
Thursday	3	10	Ascn	24	31
Friday	4	11	18	25	
Saturday	5	12	19	26	

June

		TrS	Tr1	Tr2	Tr3
Sunday					
Monday		4	11	18	25
Tuesday		5	12	19	26
Wednesday		6	13	20	27
Thursday		7	14	21	28
Friday	1	8	15	22	29
Saturday	2	9	16	23	30

July

	Tr4	Tr5	Tr6	Tr7	Tr8
Sunday					
Monday	2	9	16	23	30
Tuesday	3	10	17	24	31
Wednesday	4	11	18	25	
Thursday	5	12	19	26	
Friday	6	13	20	27	
Saturday	7	14	21	28	

August

		Tr9	Tr10	Tr11	Tr12
Sunday					
Monday		6	13	20	27
Tuesday		7	14	21	28
Wednesday	1	8	15	22	29
Thursday	2	9	16	23	30
Friday	3	10	17	24	31
Saturday	4	11	18	25	

September

		Tr13	Tr14	Tr15	Tr16	Tr17
Sunday						
Monday		3	10	17	24	
Tuesday		4	11	18	25	
Wednesday		5	12	19	26	
Thursday		6	13	20	27	
Friday		7	14	21	28	
Saturday	1	8	15	22	29	

October

		Tr18	Tr19	Tr20	LaTr
Sunday					
Monday	1	8	15	22	29
Tuesday	2	9	16	23	30
Wednesday	3	10	17	24	31
Thursday	4	11	18	25	
Friday	5	12	19	26	
Saturday	6	13	20	27	

November 2012

		4bAdv	3bAdv	2bAdv	ChrK
Sunday					
Monday		5	12	19	26
Tuesday		6	13	20	27
Wednesday		7	14	21	28
Thursday	AllSS	8	15	22	29
Friday	2	9	16	23	30
Saturday	3	10	17	24	

December 2012

		Adv1	Adv2	Adv3	Adv4	Chr1
Sunday						
Monday		3	10	17	24	31
Tuesday		4	11	18	Chr	
Wednesday		5	12	19	26	
Thursday		6	13	20	27	
Friday		7	14	21	28	
Saturday	1	8	15	22	29	

On Sunday 29 January The Presentation (Candlemas), transferred from 2 February, may be celebrated.
On Sunday 24 June The Birth of John the Baptist may be celebrated.
On Sunday 22 July Mary Magdalene may be celebrated.
On Sunday 28 October Simon and Jude, Apostles may be celebrated.
On Sunday 4 November 2012 All Saints' Day, transferred from 1 November, may be celebrated.